The Constitution of
The State of South Carolina:
A Quick Reference Guide

Bootblack Budget Books
Copyright 2018 ©
ISBN-13: 978-1722118228
ISBN-10: 1722118229

Article II: Right of Suffrage – Page 38

Article V: The Judicial Department – Page 64

Article VI: Officers – Page 73

Article VII: Counties and County Government – Page 77

Article VIII: Local Government – Page 82

Section 1. Powers of Political Subdivisions Continued

Section 2. Boundaries of Counties

Section 3. Number of Counties

Section 4. Merger of Counties

Section 5. Merger of Parts of Counties with Adjoining Counties

Section 6. Removal of County Seat

Section 7. Organization, Power, and Duties of Counties; Special Laws Prohibited

Section 8. Incorporation of New Municipalities; Readjustment of Municipal Boundaries; Merger of Municipalities; Special Laws Prohibited

Section 9. Organization, Powers, and Duties of Municipalities

Section 10. Law or Exemption for a Specific Municipality Prohibited

Section 11. Adoption and Amendment of Municipal Charters

Section 12. Consolidation of Counties with Municipalities and Other Political Subdivisions

Section 13. Joint Administration of Functions and Exercise of Powers

Section 14. General Law Provisions Not to Be Set Aside
In enacting provisions required or authorized by this article, general law provisions applicable to the following matters shall not be set aside:

Section 15. Consent of Local Governing Body to Certain Laws Required

Section 16. Acquisition and Operation of Public Utility Systems

Section 17. Construction of Constitution and Laws

Section 18. Assignment and Regulation of Territories for Electrical and Gas Utilities

Article VIII-A: Alcoholic Liquor and Beverages – Page 90

Section 1. Powers of General Assembly

Article IX: Corporations – Page 91

Section 1. Regulation of Common Carriers, Publicly-Owned

Section 2. Formation, Organization, and Regulation of Corporations

Article X: Finance, Taxation and Bonded Debt – Page 92

Section 1. Taxation and Assessment

Section 2. Defining Classes of Property and Values for Property Tax Purposes; Transition to Assessment Ratios; Continuance of Existing Statutes Pertaining to Assessment Methods; Changing Assessment Ratios

Section 3. Property Exempt from Ad Valorem Taxation

Section 4. One Assessment for All Taxes

Section 5. No Tax without Consent; Taxes to Be Levied in Pursuance of Law

Section 6. Establishment of Method of Valuation for Assessment of Real Property within State

Section 7. Limitation on Annual Expenditures of State Government and Number of State Employees; Annual Budgets and Expenses of Political Subdivisions and School Districts

Section 8. Payments from Treasuries

Section 9. Statement of Receipts and Expenditures

Section 10. Claims Against State

Section 11. Credit of State and Political Subdivisions

Section 12. Counties Not to Incur Bonded Indebtedness for Special Services in Certain Areas without Special Tax or Charge on Area or Persons Benefited

Section 13. Bonded Indebtedness of State

Section 14. Bonded Indebtedness of Political Subdivisions

Section 15. Bonded Indebtedness of School Districts

Section 16. Regulation of Benefits, Funding and Membership Contributions of State-Operated Retirement Systems; Investment of Funds

Article XI: Public Education – Page 114

Section 1. State Board of Education

Section 2. State Superintendent of Education

Section 3. System of Free Public Schools and Other Public Institutions of Learning

Section 4. Direct Aid to Religious or Other Private Educational Institutions Prohibited

Article XIII: Militia – Page 117

Article XIV: Eminent Domain – Page 119

Section 1. Boundary Rivers

Section 2. Title to Certain Lands

Section 3. Ultimate Property in Lands

Section 4. Navigable Waters Free; Tax for Use of Wharf

Section 5. Reserved

Article XV: Impeachment – Page 120

Section 1. Power of Impeachment; Vote Required; Suspension of Officer Impeached

Section 2. Trial of Impeachments; Judgment; Proceedings No Bar to Criminal Prosecution; Impeachment of Governor

Section 3. Removal of Officers by Governor on Address of General Assembly

Article XVI: Amendment and Revision of the Constitution – Page 122

Section 1. Amendments

Section 2. Two or More Amendments

Section 3. Constitutional Convention

Section 14. Citizens Deemed Sui Juris; Restrictions as to Sale of Alcoholic Beverages

Section 15. Lawful Domestic Unions Recognizable in State; Domestic Unions Created in Another Jurisdiction

Preamble:

We, the people of the State of South Carolina, in Convention assembled, grateful to God for our liberties, do ordain and establish this Constitution for the preservation and perpetuation of the same.

ARTICLE I: DECLARATION OF RIGHTS

Section 1: Political Power in People

All political power is vested in and derived from the people only, therefore, they have the right at all times to modify their form of government.

Section 2. Religious Freedom; Freedom of Speech; Right of Assembly and Petition

The General Assembly shall make no law respecting an establishment of religion or prohibiting the free exercise thereof, or abridging the freedom of speech or of the press; or the right of the people peaceably to assemble and to petition the government or any department thereof for a redress of grievances.

Section 3. Privileges and Immunities; Due Process; Equal Protection of Laws

The privileges and immunities of citizens of this State and of the United States under this Constitution shall not be abridged, nor shall any person be deprived of life, liberty, or property without due process of law, nor shall any person be denied the equal protection of the laws.

Section 4. Attainder; Ex Post Facto Laws; Impairment of Contracts; Titles; Effect of Conviction

No bill of attainder, ex post facto law, law impairing the obligation of contracts, nor law granting any title of nobility or hereditary emolument, shall be passed, and no conviction shall work corruption of blood or forfeiture of estate.

Section 5. Elections, Free and Open

All elections shall be free and open, and every inhabitant of this State possessing the qualifications provided for in this Constitution shall have an equal right to elect officers and be elected to fill public office.

Section 6. Residence

Temporary absence from the State shall not forfeit a residence once obtained.

Section 7. Suspension of Laws

The power to suspend the laws shall be exercised only by the General Assembly or by its authority in particular cases expressly provided for by it.

Section 8. Separation of Powers

In the government of this State, the legislative, executive, and judicial powers of the government shall be forever separate and distinct from each other, and no person or persons exercising the functions of one of said departments shall assume or discharge the duties of any other.

Section 9. Courts; Speedy Remedy

All courts shall be public, and every person shall have speedy remedy therein for wrongs sustained.

Section 10. Searches and Seizures; Invasions of Privacy

The right of the people to be secure in their persons, houses, papers, and effects against unreasonable searches and seizures and unreasonable invasions of privacy shall not be violated, and no warrants shall issue but upon probable cause, supported by oath or affirmation, and particularly describing the place to be searched, the person or thing to be seized, and the information to be obtained.

Section 11. Presentment or Indictment

No person may be held to answer for any crime the jurisdiction over which is not within the magistrate's court, unless on a presentment or indictment of a grand jury of the county where the crime has been committed, except in cases arising in the land or naval forces or in the militia when in actual service in time of war or public danger. The General Assembly may provide for the waiver of an indictment by the accused. Nothing contained in this Constitution is deemed to limit or prohibit the establishment by the General Assembly of a state grand jury with the authority to return indictments irrespective of the county where the crime has been committed and that other authority, including procedure, as the General Assembly may provide.

Section 12. Double Jeopardy; Self-Incrimination

No person shall be subject for the same offense to be twice put in jeopardy of life or liberty, nor shall any person be compelled in any criminal case to be a witness against himself.

Section 13. Taking Private Property; Economic Development; Remedy of Blight

(A) Except as otherwise provided in this Constitution, private property shall not be taken for private use without the consent of the owner, nor for public use without just compensation being first made for the property. Private property must not be condemned by eminent domain for any purpose or benefit including, but not limited to, the purpose or benefit of economic development, unless the condemnation is for public use.

(B) For the limited purpose of the remedy of blight, the General Assembly may provide by law that private property constituting a danger to the safety and health of the community by reason of lack of ventilation, light, and sanitary facilities, dilapidation, deleterious land use, or any combination of these factors may be condemned by eminent domain without the consent of the owner and put to a public use or private use if just compensation is first made for the property.

Section 14. Trial by Jury; Witnesses; Defense

The right of trial by jury shall be preserved inviolate. Any person charged with an offense shall enjoy the right to a speedy and public trial by an impartial jury; to be fully informed of the nature and cause of the accusation; to be confronted with the witnesses against him; to have compulsory process for obtaining witnesses in his favor, and to be fully heard in his defense by himself or by his counsel or by both.

Section 15. Right of Bail; Excessive Bail; Cruel or Unusual or Corporal Punishment; Detention of Witnesses

All persons shall be, before conviction, bailable by sufficient sureties, but bail may be denied to persons charged with capital offenses or offenses punishable by life imprisonment, or with violent offenses defined by the General Assembly, giving due weight to the evidence and to the nature and circumstances of the event. Excessive bail shall not be required, nor shall excessive fines be imposed, nor shall cruel, nor corporal, nor unusual punishment be inflicted, nor shall witnesses be unreasonably detained.

Section 16. Libel

In all indictments or prosecutions for libel, the truth of the alleged libel may be given in evidence, and the jury shall be the judges of the law and facts.

Section 17. Treason

Treason against the State shall consist alone in levying war or in giving aid and comfort to enemies against the State. No person shall be held guilty of treason, except upon testimony of at least two witnesses to the same overt act, or upon confession in open court.

Section 18. Suspension of Habeas Corpus

The privilege of the writ of habeas corpus shall not be suspended unless when, in case of insurrection, rebellion or invasion, the public safety may require it.

Section 19. Imprisonment for Debt

No person shall be imprisoned for debt except in cases of fraud.

Section 20. Right to Keep and Bear Arms; Armies; Military Power Subordinate to Civil Authority; How Soldiers Quartered

A well regulated militia being necessary to the security of a free State, the right of the people to keep and bear arms shall not be infringed. As, in times of peace, armies are dangerous to liberty, they shall not be maintained without the consent of the General Assembly. The military power of the State shall always be held in subordination to the civil authority and be governed by it. No soldier shall in time of peace be quartered in any house without the consent of the owner nor in time of war but in the manner prescribed by law.

Section 21. Martial Law

No person shall in any case be subject to martial law or to any pains or penalties by virtue of that law, except those employed in the armed forces of the United States, and except the militia in actual service, but by the authority of the General Assembly.

Section 22. Procedure Before Administrative Agencies; Judicial Review

No person shall be finally bound by a judicial or quasi-judicial decision of an administrative agency affecting private rights except on due notice and an opportunity to be heard; nor shall he be subject to the same person for both prosecution and adjudication; nor shall he be deprived of liberty or property unless by a mode of procedure prescribed by the General Assembly, and he shall have in all such instances the right to judicial review.

Section 23. Provisions of Constitution Mandatory

The provisions of the Constitution shall be taken, deemed, and construed to be mandatory and prohibitory, and not merely directory, except where expressly made directory or permissory by its own terms.

Section 24. Victims' Bill of Rights

(A) To preserve and protect victims' rights to justice and due process regardless of race, sex, age, religion, or economic status, victims of crime have the right to:

(1) be treated with fairness, respect, and dignity, and to be free from intimidation, harassment, or abuse, throughout the criminal and juvenile justice process, and informed of the victim's constitutional rights, provided by statute;

(2) be reasonably informed when the accused or convicted person is arrested, released from custody, or has escaped;

(3) be informed of and present at any criminal proceedings which are dispositive of the charges where the defendant has the right to be present;

(4) be reasonably informed of and be allowed to submit either a written or oral statement at all hearings affecting bond or bail;

(5) be heard at any proceeding involving a post-arrest release decision, a plea, or sentencing;

(6) be reasonably protected from the accused or persons acting on his behalf throughout the criminal justice process;

(7) confer with the prosecution, after the crime against the victim has been charged, before the trial or before any disposition and informed of the disposition;

(8) have reasonable access after the conclusion of the criminal investigation to all documents relating to the crime against the victim before trial;

(9) receive prompt and full restitution from the person or persons convicted of the criminal conduct that caused the victim's loss or injury, including both adult and juvenile offenders;

(10) be informed of any proceeding when any post-conviction action is being considered, and be present at any post-conviction hearing involving a post-conviction release decision;

(11) a reasonable disposition and prompt and final conclusion of the case;

(12) have all rules governing criminal procedure and the admissibility of evidence in all criminal proceedings protect victims' rights and have these rules subject to amendment or repeal by the legislature to ensure protection of these rights.

(B) Nothing in this section creates a civil cause of action on behalf of any person against any public employee, public agency, the State, or any agency responsible for the enforcement of rights and provision of services contained in this section. The rights created in this section may be subject to a writ of mandamus, to be issued by any justice of the Supreme Court or circuit court judge to require compliance by any public employee, public agency, the State, or any agency responsible for the enforcement of the rights and provisions of these services contained in this section, and a wilful failure to comply with a writ of mandamus is punishable as contempt.

(C) For purposes of this section:

(1) A victim's exercise of any right granted by this section is not grounds for dismissing any criminal proceeding or setting aside any conviction or sentence.

(2) "Victim" means a person who suffers direct or threatened physical, psychological, or financial harm as the result of the commission or attempted commission of a crime against him. The term "victim" also includes the person's spouse, parent, child, or lawful representative of a crime victim who is deceased, who is a minor or who is incompetent or who was a homicide victim or who is physically or psychologically incapacitated.

(3) The General Assembly has the authority to enact substantive and procedural laws to define, implement, preserve, and protect the rights guaranteed to victims by this section, including the authority to extend any of these rights to juvenile proceedings.

(4) The enumeration in the Constitution of certain rights for victims shall not be construed to deny or disparage others granted by the General Assembly or retained by victims. Amendments

Section 25. Right to Hunt and Fish

The traditions of hunting and fishing are valuable parts of the state's heritage, important for conservation, and a protected means of managing nonthreatened wildlife. The citizens of this State have the right to hunt, fish, and harvest wildlife traditionally pursued, subject to laws and regulations promoting sound wildlife conservation and management as prescribed by the General Assembly. Nothing in this section shall be construed to abrogate any private property rights, existing state laws or regulations, or the state's sovereignty over its natural resources."

ARTICLE II: RIGHT OF SUFFERAGE

Section 1. Elections to Be by Secret Ballot; Protection of Right of Suffrage

All elections by the people shall be by secret ballot, but the ballots shall not be counted in secret. The right of suffrage, as regulated in this Constitution, shall be protected by laws regulating elections and prohibiting, under adequate penalties, all undue influence from power, bribery, tumult, or improper conduct.

Section 2. Free Exercise of Right of Suffrage

No power, civil or military, shall at any time interfere to prevent the free exercise of the right of suffrage in this State.

Section 3. Electors

Every citizen possessing the qualifications required by this Constitution and not laboring under the disabilities named in or authorized by it shall be an elector.

Section 4. Voter Qualifications

Every citizen of the United States and of this State of the age of eighteen and upwards who is properly registered is entitled to vote as provided by law.

Section 5. Qualifications of Municipal Electors

Municipal electors shall possess the qualifications prescribed in this Constitution, but each such elector must have resided in the municipality in which he offers to vote for thirty days next preceding the election.

Section 6. General Assembly May Require Demonstration of Literacy

The General Assembly may require each person to demonstrate a reasonable ability, except for physical disability, to read and write the English language as a condition to becoming entitled to vote.

Section 7. Disqualifications by Reason of Mental Incompetence or Conviction of Crime

The General Assembly shall establish disqualifications for voting by reason of mental incompetence or conviction of serious crime, and may provide for the removal of such disqualifications. Persons who are confined in any penal institution under the judgment of a court shall not be entitled to vote.

Section 8. Registration of Voters

The General Assembly shall provide for the registration of voters for periods not less than ten years in duration. Provision shall be made for registration during every year for persons entitled to be registered. The registration lists shall be public records.

Section 9. Appeal by Person Denied Registration

Any person denied registration shall have the right to appeal to the court of common pleas, or any judge thereof, and thence to the Supreme Court, to determine his right to vote under the limitations imposed in or authorized by this article, and on such appeal the hearing shall be de novo, and the General Assembly shall provide for such appeal.

Section 10. Nominations; Conduct of Elections; Contests

The General Assembly shall provide for the nomination of candidates, regulate the time, place and manner of elections, provide for the administration of elections and for absentee voting, insure secrecy of voting, establish procedures for contested elections, and enact other provisions necessary to the fulfillment and integrity of the election process.

Section 11. Electors Privileged from Arrest

Electors shall in all cases except treason, felony, or a breach of the peace, be privileged from arrest on the days of election during their attendance at the polls for voting, and going to and returning therefrom.

Section 12. Right to Vote by Secret Ballot

The fundamental right of an individual to vote by secret ballot is guaranteed for a designation, a selection, or an authorization for employee representation by a labor organization.

ARTICLE III: LEGISLATIVE DEPARTMENT

Section 1. Legislative Power Vested in Two Branches

The legislative power of this State shall be vested in two distinct branches, the one to be styled the "Senate" and the other the "House of Representatives," and both together the "General Assembly of the State of South Carolina."

Section 1A. Meeting of General Assembly

The General Assembly ought frequently to assemble for the redress of grievances and for making new laws, as the common good may require.

Section 2. House of Representatives

The House of Representatives shall be composed of members chosen by ballot every second year by citizens of this State, qualified as in this Constitution is provided.

Section 3. Number of Members; Enumeration of Inhabitants

The House of Representatives shall consist of one hundred and twenty-four members, to be apportioned among the several Counties according to the number of inhabitants contained in each. Each County shall constitute one election district. An enumeration of the inhabitants for this purpose shall be made in the year Nineteen hundred and One, and shall be made in the course of every tenth year thereafter, in such manner as shall be by law directed: Provided, That the General Assembly may at any time, in its discretion, adopt the immediately preceding United States Census as a true and correct enumeration of the inhabitants of the several Counties, and make the apportionment of Representatives among the several Counties, according to said enumeration: Provided, further, That until the apportionment which shall be made upon the next enumeration shall take effect, the representation of the several Counties as they now exist (including the County of Saluda established by ordinance) shall be as follows:

Abbeville, 5;

Aiken, 3;

Anderson, 5;

Barnwell, 5;

Beaufort, 4;

Berkeley, 4;

Charleston, 9;

Chester, 3;

Chesterfield, 2;

Clarendon, 3;

Colleton, 4;

Darlington, 3;

Edgefield, 3;

Fairfield, 3;

Florence, 3;

Georgetown, 2;

Greenville, 5;

Hampton, 2;

Horry, 2;

Kershaw, 2;

Lancaster, 2;

Laurens, 3;

 Lexington, 2;

Marion, 3;

Marlboro, 3;

Newberry, 3;

Oconee, 2;

Orangeburg, 5;

Pickens, 2;

Richland, 4;

Saluda, 2;

Spartanburg, 6;

Sumter, 5;

Union, 3;

Williamsburg, 3;

York, 4;

Provided further, That in the event other Counties are hereafter established, then the General Assembly shall reapportion the Representatives between the Counties.

Section 4. Assignment of Representatives

In assigning Representatives to the several Counties, the General Assembly shall allow one Representative to every one hundred and twenty-fourth part of the whole number of inhabitants in the State: Provided, That if in the apportionment of Representatives any County shall appear not to be entitled, from its population, to a Representative, such County shall, nevertheless, send one Representative; and if there be still a deficiency in the number of Representatives required by Section third of this Article, such deficiency shall be supplied by assigning Representatives to those Counties having the largest surplus fractions.

Section 5. When Apportionment Takes Effect

No apportionment of Representatives shall take effect until the general election which shall succeed such apportionment.

Section 6. Senate

The Senate shall be composed of one member from each County, to be elected for the term of four years by the qualified electors in each County, in the same manner in which members of the House of Representatives are chosen.

Section 7. Qualifications of Members of Senate and House of Representatives

No person is eligible for a seat in the Senate or House of Representatives who, at the time of his election, is not a duly qualified elector under this Constitution in the district in which he may be chosen. Senators must be at least twenty-five and Representatives at least twenty-one years of age. A candidate for the Senate or House of Representatives must be a legal resident of the district in which he is a candidate at the time he files for the office. No person who has been convicted of a felony under state or federal law or convicted of tampering with a voting machine, fraudulent registration or voting, bribery at elections, procuring or offering to procure votes by bribery, voting more than once at elections, impersonating a voter, or swearing falsely at elections/taking oath in another's name, or who has pled guilty or nolo contendere to these offenses, is eligible to serve as a member of the Senate or the House of Representatives. However, notwithstanding any other provision of this Constitution, this prohibition does not apply to a person who has been pardoned under state or federal law or to a person who files for public office fifteen years or more after the completion date of service of the sentence, including probation and parole time, nor shall any person, serving in office prior to the ratification of this provision, be required to vacate the office to which he is elected.

Section 8. Election of Representatives

The first election for members of the House of Representatives under this Constitution shall be held on Tuesday after the first Monday in November Eighteen Hundred and Ninety-six, and in every second year thereafter, in such manner and at such places as the General Assembly may prescribe.

Section 9. Sessions of General Assembly

The annual session of the General Assembly shall convene at the State Capitol Building in the City of Columbia on the second Tuesday of January of each year. After the convening of the General Assembly, nothing in this section shall prohibit the Senate or the House of Representatives, or both, from receding for a time period not to exceed thirty consecutive calendar days at a time by a majority vote of the members of the body of the General Assembly seeking to recede for a time period not to exceed thirty consecutive calendar days, or from receding for a time period of more than thirty consecutive calendar days at a time by a two-thirds vote of the members of the body of the General Assembly seeking to recede for more than thirty consecutive calendar days at a time. Each body shall sit in session at the State Capitol Building in the City of Columbia and may provide for meetings during the legislative session as it shall consider appropriate. Furthermore, the Senate or the House of Representatives, or both, may meet on the first Tuesday following the certification of the election of its members for not more than three days following the general election in even-numbered years for the purpose of organizing. If the casualties of war or contagious disease render it unsafe to meet at the seat of government, the Governor, by proclamation, may appoint a more secure and convenient place of meeting. Members of the General Assembly shall not receive any compensation for more than forty days of any one session.

Section 10. Terms of Office

The terms of office of the Senators and Representatives chosen at a general election shall begin on the Monday following such election.

Section 11. Election Returns; Quorum; Absent Members
Each house shall judge of the election returns and qualifications of its own members, and a majority of each house shall constitute a quorum to do business; but a smaller number may adjourn from day to day, and may compel the attendance of absent members, in such manner and under such penalties as may be provided by law or rule.

Section 12. Officers; Rules; Punishment and Expulsion of Members

Each house shall choose its own officers, determine its rules of procedure, punish its members for disorderly behavior, and, with the concurrence of two-thirds, expel a member, but not a second time for the same cause.

Section 13. Punishment of Persons Not Members

Each house may punish by imprisonment during its sitting any person not a member who shall be guilty of disrespect to the house by any disorderly or contemptuous behavior in its presence, or who, during the time of its sitting, shall threaten harm to the body or estate of any member for anything said or done in either house, or who shall assault any of them therefore, or who shall assault or arrest any witness or other person ordered to attend the house in his going thereto or returning therefrom, or who shall rescue any person arrested by order of the house: Provided, That such time of imprisonment shall not in any case extend beyond the session of the General Assembly.

Section 14. Members in Attendance Protected

The members of both houses shall be protected in their persons and estates during their attendance on, going to and returning from the General Assembly, and ten days previous to the sitting and ten days after the adjournment thereof. But these privileges shall not protect any member who shall be charged with treason, felony or breach of the peace.

Section 15. Bills for Revenue; Other Bills

Bills for raising revenue shall originate in the House of Representatives, but may be altered, amended or rejected by the Senate; all other Bills may originate in either house, and may be amended, altered or rejected by the other.

Section 16. Style of Laws

The style of all laws shall be: "Be it enacted by the General Assembly of the State of South Carolina."

Section 17. One Subject

Every Act or resolution having the force of law shall relate to but one subject, and that shall be expressed in the title.

Section 18. Formalities of Act

No Bill or Joint Resolution shall have the force of law until it shall have been read three times and on three several days in each house, has had the Great Seal of the State affixed to it, and has been signed by the President of the Senate and the Speaker of the House of Representatives: Provided, That either branch of the General Assembly may provide by rule for a first and third reading of any Bill or Joint Resolution by its title only.

Section 19. Mileage; Increase of Per Diem; Compensation during Extra Session

Each member of the General Assembly shall receive such mileage allowance for the ordinary route of travel in going to and returning from the place where its sessions are held as the General Assembly may provide by law; no General Assembly shall have the power to increase the per diem of its own members; and members of the General Assembly when convened in extra session shall receive the same compensation as is fixed by law for the regular session.

Section 20. Elections "Viva Voce"

In all elections by the General Assembly or either House thereof, the members shall vote "viva voce," except by unanimous consent, and their votes thus given shall be entered upon the Journal of the House to which they respectively belong.

Section 21. Deleted

Section 22. Journal; Yeas and Nays

Each house shall keep a journal of its own proceedings, and cause the same to be published immediately after its adjournment, excepting such parts as, in its judgment, may require secrecy; and the yeas and nays of the members of either house, on any question, shall, at the desire of ten members of the House or five members of the Senate, respectively, be entered on the journal. Any member of either house shall have liberty to dissent from and protest against any Act or resolution which he may think injurious to the public or to an individual, and have the reasons of his dissent entered on the journal.

Section 23. Doors Open

The doors of each house shall be open, except on such occasions as in the opinion of the House may require secrecy.

Section 24. Dual Office Holding

No person is eligible to a seat in the General Assembly while he holds any office or position of profit or trust under this State, the United States of America, or any of them, or under any other power, except officers in the militia, members of lawfully and regularly organized fire departments, constables, and notaries public. If any member accepts or exercises any of the disqualifying offices or positions he shall vacate his seat.

Section 25. Vacancies

If any election district shall neglect to choose a member or members on the day of election, or if any person chosen a member of either house shall refuse to qualify and take his seat, or shall resign, die, depart the State, accept any disqualifying office or position, or become otherwise disqualified to hold his seat, a writ of election shall be issued by the President of the

Senate or Speaker of the House of Representatives, as the case may be, for the purpose of filling the vacancy thereby occasioned for the remainder of the term for which the person so refusing to qualify, resigning, dying, departing the State, or becoming disqualified, was elected to serve, or the defaulting election district ought to have chosen a member or members.

Section 26. Oath of Office

Members of the General Assembly, and all officers, before they enter upon the duties of their respective offices, and all members of the bar, before they enter upon the practice of their profession, shall take and subscribe the following oath: "I do solemnly swear (or affirm) that I am duly qualified, according to the Constitution of this State, to exercise the duties of the office to which I have been elected, (or appointed), and that I will, to the best of my ability, discharge the duties thereof, and preserve, protect and defend the Constitution of this State and of the United States. So help me God."

Section 27. Removal of Officer

Officers shall be removed for incapacity, misconduct or neglect of duty, in such manner as may be provided by law, when no mode of trial or removal is provided in this Constitution.

Section 28. Debtor's Exemption from Attachment, Levy, and Sale

The General Assembly shall enact such laws as will exempt real and personal property of a debtor from attachment, levy and sale under any mesne or final process issued by any court or bankruptcy proceeding.

Section 29. Determining Personal and Real Property Taxes

Taxes on personal property must be laid upon the actual value of the property taxed, as the same shall be ascertained by an assessment made for the purpose of laying such tax. Taxes on real property must be ascertained by the methods provided by the General Assembly by general law as prescribed in Article X of this Constitution.

Section 30. Extra Compensation Not Permitted; Appropriations for Repelling Invasion

The General Assembly shall never grant extra compensation, fee or allowance to any public officer, agent, servant or contractor after service rendered, or contract made, nor authorize payment or part payment of any claim under any contract not authorized by law; but appropriations may be made for expenditures in repelling invasion, preventing or suppressing insurrection.

Section 31. Public Lands

Lands belonging to or under the control of the State shall never be donated, directly or indirectly, to private corporations or individuals, or to railroad companies. Nor shall such land be sold to corporations, or associations, for a less price than that for which it can be sold to individuals. This, however, shall not prevent the General Assembly from granting a right of way, not exceeding one hundred and fifty feet in width, as a mere easement to railroads across State land, nor to interfere with the discretion of the General Assembly in confirming the title to lands claimed to belong to the State, but used or possessed by other parties under an adverse claim.

Section 32. Deleted

Section 33. Age of Consent

No unmarried woman shall legally consent to sexual intercourse who shall not have attained the age of fourteen years.

Section 34. Special Laws Prohibited

The General Assembly of this State shall not enact local or special laws concerning any of the following subjects or for any of the following purposes, to wit:

I. To change the names of persons or places.

II. To incorporate cities, towns or villages, or change, amend or extend charter thereof.

III. To incorporate educational, religious, charitable, social, manufacturing or banking institutions not under the control of the State, or amend or extend the charters thereof.

IV. To incorporate school districts.

V. To authorize the adoption or legitimation of children.

VI. To provide for the protection of game.

VII. To summon and empanel grand or petit jurors; provided, that tales boxes may be eliminated by special act in York County.

VIII. Eliminated

IX. In all other cases, where a general law can be made applicable, no special law shall be enacted: Provided, That the General Assembly may enact local or special laws fixing the amount and manner of compensation to be paid to the County Officers of the several counties of the State, and may provide that the fees collected by any such officer, or officers, shall be paid into the treasury of the respective counties.

X. The General Assembly shall forthwith enact general laws concerning said subjects for said purposes, which shall be uniform in their operations: Provided, That nothing contained in this section shall prohibit the General Assembly from enacting special provisions in general laws.

XI. The provisions of this Section shall not apply to charitable and educational corporations where, under the terms of a gift, devise or will, special incorporation may be required.

Provided, That the General Assembly is empowered to divide the State into as many zones as may appear practicable, and to enact legislation as may appear proper for the protection of game in the several zones.

Provided, further, that the General Assembly is empowered to divide the State into as many districts as may appear practicable, and to enact legislation as may appear proper for the protection of forestry in the several districts.

Provided, there is hereby created a civil service commission in the City of Spartanburg for the benefit of the police department, including its chief, and fire department, including its chief, under such terms and conditions as prescribed by the General Assembly.

Provided, that the City of Gaffney may establish a civil service commission for the benefit of such municipal employees as may be designated by the Gaffney City Council, under such terms and conditions as prescribed by the General Assembly.

Section 35. Lands Owned by Aliens

It shall be the duty of the General Assembly to enact laws limiting the number of acres of land which any alien or any corporation controlled by aliens may own within this State.

Section 36. General Reserve Fund

(A) The General Assembly shall provide for a General Reserve Fund of five percent of the general fund revenue of the latest completed fiscal year. The five percent requirement shall be reached by adding a cumulative one-half of one percent of such revenue in each fiscal year succeeding the last fiscal year to which the three percent applied until the percentage of such revenues equals five percent which shall then and thereafter apply unless adjusted as provided in this section. The percentage amount required by this subsection may be increased or decreased by legislative enactment passed by a two-thirds vote of the total membership of the Senate and a two-thirds vote of the total membership of the House of Representatives, with the yeas and nays recorded in the respective journal of each house. The legislation must be separate and enacted solely for the purpose of increasing or decreasing the percentage amount. Funds may be withdrawn from the reserve only for the purpose of covering operating deficits of state government. The General Assembly must provide for the orderly restoration of funds withdrawn from the reserve from future revenues and out of funds accumulating in excess of annual operating expenditures.

(1) The General Assembly shall provide by law for a procedure to survey the progress of the collection of revenue and the expenditure of funds and to authorize and direct reduction of appropriations as may be necessary to prevent a deficit. (2) In the event of a year-end operating deficit, so much of the reserve fund as may be necessary must be used to cover the deficit; and the amount must be restored to the reserve fund within five fiscal years out of future revenues until the five percent, or the applicable percentage amount required to be transferred to the General Reserve Fund, is again reached and maintained. Provided that a minimum of one percent of the general fund revenue of the latest completed fiscal year, if so much is necessary, must be restored to the reserve fund each year following the deficit until the five percent, or the applicable percentage amount required by general law to be transferred to the General Reserve Fund is restored.

(B) The General Assembly, in the annual general appropriations act, shall appropriate, out of the estimated revenue of the general fund for the fiscal year for which the appropriations are made, into a Capital Reserve Fund, which is separate and distinct from the General Reserve Fund, an amount equal to two percent of the general fund revenue of the latest completed fiscal year.

(1) The General Assembly must provide by law that if before March first the revenue forecast for the current fiscal year projects that revenues at the end of the fiscal year will be less than expenditures authorized by appropriation for that year, then the current year's appropriation to the Capital Reserve Fund first must be reduced to the extent necessary before mandating any reductions in operating appropriations.

(2) After March first of a fiscal year, monies from the Capital Reserve Fund may be appropriated by the General Assembly in separate legislation upon an affirmative vote in each branch of the General Assembly by two-thirds of the members present and voting, but not less than three-fifths of the total membership in each branch for the following purposes:

(a) to finance in cash previously authorized capital improvement bond projects;

(b) to retire interest or principal on bonds previously issued;

(c) for capital improvements or other nonrecurring purposes.

(3)

(a) Any appropriation of monies from the Capital Reserve Fund as provided in this subsection must be ranked in priority of expenditure and is effective thirty days after completion of the fiscal year. If it is determined that the fiscal year has ended with an operating deficit, then the monies appropriated from the

Capital Reserve Fund must be reduced based on the rank of priority, beginning with the lowest priority, to the extent necessary and applied to the year-end operating deficit before withdrawing monies from the General Reserve Fund.

(b) At the end of the fiscal year, any monies in the Capital Reserve Fund that are not appropriated as provided in this subsection or any appropriation for a particular project or item which has been reduced due to application of the monies to a year-end deficit must lapse and be credited to the General Fund.

Section 37. President of Senate

The Senate shall, as soon as practicable after the convening of the General Assembly in 2019 and every four years thereafter, elect from among the members thereof a President to preside over the Senate and to perform other duties as provided by law.

ARTICLE IV: EXECUTIVE DEPARTMENT

Section 1. Chief Magistrate

The supreme executive authority of this State shall be vested in a Chief Magistrate, who shall be styled "The Governor of the State of South Carolina."

Section 2. Qualifications of Governor

No person shall be eligible to the office of Governor who denies the existence of the Supreme Being; and who on the date of such election has not attained the age of thirty years; and who shall not have been a citizen of the United States and a citizen and resident of this State for five years next preceding the day of election. No person while Governor shall hold any office or other commission (except in the militia) under the authority of this State, or of any other power.

Section 3. Election of Governor; Governor May Not Serve More Than Two Successive Terms

The Governor shall be elected by the qualified voters of the State at the regular election every other even-numbered year after 1970. No person shall be elected Governor for more than two successive terms.

Section 4. Term of Governor

The term of office of the Governor shall be four years, beginning at noon on the first Wednesday following the second Tuesday in January next after his election and ending at noon on the first Wednesday following the second Tuesday in January four years later.

Section 5. Person Having Highest Number of Votes to Be Governor; Tie Vote

In the general election for Governor, the person having the highest number of votes shall be Governor. In the event of a tie vote, as the first order of business after its organization, the General Assembly in joint session shall elect the Governor from the candidates having received the tie vote by the affirmative vote of a majority of the combined membership of both houses.

Section 6. Succession When Governor-Elect Dies, Declines to Serve, or Fails to Take Oath

If the Governor-elect dies or declines to serve, the Lieutenant Governor-elect shall become Governor for a full term. If the Governor-elect fails to take the oath of office at the commencement of his term, the Lieutenant Governor shall act as Governor until the oath is administered.

Section 7. Succession When Neither Governor-Elect nor Lieutenant Governor-Elect Qualifies or Is Able to Serve

In the event that neither the Governor-elect nor the Lieutenant Governor-elect shall qualify, or if after taking the oath of office neither shall be able to serve for any reason whatsoever, the office of Governor for the time being shall devolve upon such officers and in such order of succession as may be provided by law. Any such officers while exercising the powers of the Governor for the time being under this provision shall not be subject to the dual office-holding provision of this Constitution.

Section 8. Election, Qualifications, and Term of Lieutenant Governor

(A) A Lieutenant Governor must be chosen at the same time, in the same manner, continue in office for the same period, and be possessed of the same qualifications as the Governor.

(B) Beginning with the general election of 2018, a person seeking the office of Governor in any manner that a person's name may appear on the ballot as a candidate for that office, and before that person's name is certified to appear on the ballot for the general election, shall select a qualified elector to serve as Lieutenant Governor.

(C) All candidates for the offices of Governor and Lieutenant Governor must be elected jointly in a manner prescribed by law so that each voter casts a single vote to elect a candidate for the office of Governor and Lieutenant Governor.

(D) The General Assembly shall provide by law the manner in which a candidate for Lieutenant Governor is selected."

Section 9. Repealed

Section 10. Lieutenant Governor to Be President of Senate

Repealed

Section 11. Death, Resignation, Removal of Governor

In the case of the removal of the Governor from office by impeachment, death, resignation, disqualification, disability, or removal from the State, the Lieutenant Governor shall be Governor. In case the Governor be impeached, the Lieutenant Governor shall act in his stead and have his powers until judgment in the case shall have been pronounced. In the case of the temporary disability of the Governor and in the event of the temporary absence of the Governor from the State, the Lieutenant Governor shall have full authority to act in an emergency. In the case of the removal of the Lieutenant Governor from office by impeachment, death, resignation, disqualification, disability, or removal from the State, the Governor shall appoint, with the advice and consent of the Senate, a successor to fulfill the unexpired term.

Section 12. Disability of Governor

(1) Whenever the Governor transmits to the President of the Senate and the Speaker of the House of Representatives his written declaration that he is unable to discharge the powers and duties of his office, and until he transmits to them a written declaration to the contrary, such powers and duties shall be discharged by the Lieutenant Governor as acting Governor.

(2) Whenever a majority of the Attorney General, the Secretary of State, the Comptroller General and the State Treasurer, or of such other body as the General Assembly may provide, transmits to the President of the Senate and the Speaker of the House of Representatives a written declaration that the Governor is unable to discharge the powers and duties of his office, the Lieutenant Governor shall forthwith assume the powers and duties of the office as acting Governor.

Thereafter, if the Governor transmits to the President of the Senate and the Speaker of the House of Representatives his written declaration that no such inability exists he shall forthwith resume the powers and duties of his office unless a majority of the above members or of such other body, whichever the case may be, transmits within four days to the President of the Senate and the Speaker of the House of Representatives their written declaration that the Governor is unable to discharge the powers and duties of his office. Thereupon, the General Assembly shall forthwith consider and decide the issue, and if not in session it shall assemble within forty-eight hours for the sole purpose of deciding such issue. If the General Assembly, within twenty-one days, excluding Sundays, after the first day it meets to decide the issue, determines by two-thirds vote of each House that the Governor is unable to discharge the powers and duties of his office, the Lieutenant Governor shall continue to discharge the same as acting Governor; otherwise, the Governor shall resume the powers and duties of his office.

Section 13. Commander-in-Chief

The Governor shall be Commander-in-Chief of the organized and unorganized militia of the State.

Section 14. Powers of Governor as to Clemency

With respect to clemency, the Governor shall have the power only to grant reprieves and to commute a sentence of death to that of life imprisonment. The granting of all other clemency shall be regulated and provided for by law.

Section 15. Faithful Execution of Laws

The Governor shall take care that the laws be faithfully executed. To this end, the Attorney General shall assist and represent the Governor, but such power shall not be construed to authorize any action or proceeding against the General Assembly or the Supreme Court.

Section 16. Compensation of Governor and Lieutenant Governor

The Governor and Lieutenant Governor shall receive for their services compensation, which shall be neither increased nor diminished during the period for which they shall have been elected.

Section 17. Duty of State Officers to Give Information to Governor

All State officers, agencies, and institutions within the Executive Branch shall, when required by the Governor, give him information in writing upon any subject relating to the duties and functions of their respective offices, agencies, and institutions, including itemized accounts of receipts and disbursements.

Section 18. Duty of Governor to Give Information to General Assembly

The Governor shall, from time to time, give to the General Assembly information on the condition of the State and recommend for its consideration such measures as he shall deem necessary or expedient.

Section 19. Extra Sessions; Governor May Adjourn General Assembly

The Governor may on extraordinary occasions convene the General Assembly in extra session. Should either house remain without a quorum for five days, or in case of disagreement between the two houses during any session with respect to the time of adjournment, he may adjourn them to such times as he shall think proper, not beyond the time of the annual session then next ensuing.

Section 20. Residence of Governor

The Governor shall reside at the Capital of the State except in case of epidemics, natural disaster, or the emergencies of war; but during the sittings of the General Assembly he shall reside where its sessions are held.

Section 21. Bill or Joint Resolution Must Be Signed or Vetoed by Governor

Every bill or joint resolution which shall have passed the General Assembly, except on a question of adjournment, shall, before it becomes a law, be presented to the Governor, and if he approves he shall sign it; if not, he shall return it, with his objections, to the house in which it originated, which shall enter the objections at large on its Journal and proceed to reconsider it. If after such reconsideration two-thirds of that house shall agree to pass it, it shall be sent, together with the objections, to the other house, by which it shall be reconsidered, and if approved by two-thirds of that house it shall have the same effect as if it had been signed by the Governor; but in all such cases the vote of both houses shall be taken by yeas and nays, and the names of the persons voting for and against the bill or joint resolution shall be entered on the Journals of both houses respectively.

Bills appropriating money out of the Treasury shall specify the objects and purposes for which the same are made, and appropriate to them respectively their several amounts in distinct items and sections. If the Governor shall not approve any one or more of the items or sections contained in any bill appropriating money, but shall approve of the residue thereof, it shall become a law as to the residue in like manner as if he had signed it. The Governor shall then return the bill with his objections to the items or sections of the same not approved by him to the house in which the bill originated, which house shall enter the objections at large upon its Journal and proceed to reconsider so much of the bill as is not approved by the Governor. The same proceedings shall be had in both houses in reconsidering the same as is provided in case of an entire bill returned by the Governor with his objections; and if any item or section of the bill not approved by the Governor shall be passed by two-thirds of each house of the General Assembly, it shall become a part of the law notwithstanding the objections of the Governor.

If a bill or joint resolution shall not be returned by the Governor within five days after it shall have been presented to him, Sundays excepted, it shall have the same force and effect as if he had signed it, unless the General Assembly, by adjournment, prevents return, in which case it shall have such force and effect unless returned within two days after the next meeting.

ARTICLE V: THE JUDICIAL DEPARTMENT

Section 1. Judicial Power Vested in Certain Courts

The judicial power shall be vested in a unified judicial system, which shall include a Supreme Court, a Court of Appeals, a Circuit Court, and such other courts of uniform jurisdiction as may be provided for by general law.

Section 2. Supreme Court

The Supreme Court shall consist of a Chief Justice and four Associate Justices, any three of whom shall constitute a quorum for the transaction of business. The Chief Justice shall preside, and in his absence the senior Associate Justice. In all cases decided by the Supreme Court, the concurrence of three of the Justices shall be necessary for a reversal of the judgment below.

Section 3. Election of Members of Supreme Court

The members of the Supreme Court shall be elected by a joint public vote of the General Assembly for a term of ten years, and shall continue in office until their successors shall be elected and qualified, and shall be classified so that the term of one of them shall expire every two years. In any contested election, the vote of each member of the General Assembly present and voting shall be recorded.

Section 4. Powers of Chief Justice; Rules; Admission to Practice of Law and Discipline of Persons Admitted

The Chief Justice of the Supreme Court shall be the administrative head of the unified judicial system. He shall appoint an administrator of the courts and such assistants as he deems necessary to aid in the administration of the courts of the State. The Chief Justice shall set the terms of any court and shall have the power to assign any judge to sit in any court within the unified judicial system. Provided, each county shall be entitled to four weeks of court each year and such terms therefore shall be provided for by the General Assembly. Provided, further, that the Chief Justice shall set a term of at least one week in any court of original jurisdiction in any county within sixty days after receipt by him of a resolution of the county bar requesting it. The Supreme Court shall make rules governing the administration of all the courts of the State. Subject to the statutory law, the Supreme Court shall make rules governing the practice and procedure in all such courts. The Supreme Court shall have jurisdiction over the admission to the practice of law and the discipline of persons admitted.

Section 4A. Submission of Supreme Court Rules to Judiciary Committees; Disapproval by General Assembly

All rules and amendments to rules governing practice and procedure in all courts of this State promulgated by the Supreme Court must be submitted by the Supreme Court to the Judiciary Committee of each House of the General Assembly during a regular session, but not later than the first day of February during each session. Such rules or amendments shall become effective ninety calendar days after submission unless disapproved by concurrent resolution of the General Assembly, with the concurrence of three-fifths of the members of each House present and voting.

Section 5. Jurisdiction of Supreme Court

The Supreme Court shall have power to issue writs or orders of injunction, mandamus, quo warranto, prohibition, certiorari, habeas corpus, and other original and remedial writs. The Court shall have appellate jurisdiction only in cases of equity, and in such appeals they shall review the findings of fact as well as the law, except in cases where the facts are settled by a jury and the verdict not set aside. The Supreme Court shall constitute a court for the correction of errors at law under such regulations as the General Assembly may prescribe.

Section 6. Reporter and Clerk of Supreme Court

There shall be appointed by the Justices of the Supreme Court a Reporter and a Clerk of Court, whose terms and duties shall be prescribed by the Court.

Section 7. Composition and Organization of Court of Appeals; Terms of Court of Appeals

The Court of Appeals shall consist of a Chief Judge and no fewer than five Associate Judges, the appropriate number to be determined by law. The Chief Judge shall preside, and in his absence the senior Associate Judge. Subject to the supervision of the Chief Justice of the Supreme Court, the Chief Judge shall set the terms of the Court of Appeals. The structure and organization of the Court of Appeals shall be determined by the General Assembly. The Court of Appeals shall sit in panels. The General Assembly may by statute provide for the court to sit en banc.

Section 8. Election of Members of Court of Appeals

The members of the Court of Appeals shall be elected by a joint public vote of the General Assembly for a term of six years and shall continue in office until their successors shall be elected and qualify. In any contested election, the vote of each member of the General Assembly present and voting shall be recorded. Provided, that for the first election of members of the Court of Appeals, the General Assembly shall by law provide for staggered terms.

Section 9. Jurisdiction of Court of Appeals; Binding Effect of Supreme Court Decisions

The Court of Appeals shall have such jurisdiction as the General Assembly shall prescribe by general law. The decisions of the Supreme Court shall bind the Court of Appeals as precedents.

Section 10. Appointment of Clerk of Court of Appeals

There shall be appointed by the Judges of the Court of Appeals a clerk of court, whose term and duties shall be prescribed by the Court of Appeals and shall be subject to the general administrative authority and supervision of the Chief Justice.

Section 11. Jurisdiction of Circuit Court

The Circuit Court shall be a general trial court with original jurisdiction in civil and criminal cases, except those cases in which exclusive jurisdiction shall be given to inferior courts, and shall have such appellate jurisdiction as provided by law.

Section 12. Jurisdiction in Matters Testamentary and of Administration, Minors and Persons Mentally Incompetent

Jurisdiction in matters testamentary and of administration, in matters appertaining to minors and to persons mentally incompetent, shall be vested as the General Assembly may provide, consistent with the provisions of Section 1 of this article.

Section 13. Judicial Circuits

The General Assembly shall divide the State into judicial circuits of compact and contiguous territory. For each circuit a judge or judges shall be elected by a joint public vote of the General Assembly; provided, that in any contested election, the vote of each member of the General Assembly present and voting shall be recorded. He shall hold office for a term of six years, and at the time of his election he shall be an elector of a county of, and during his continuance in office he shall reside in, the circuit of which he is judge.

The General Assembly may by law provide for additional circuit judges, to be assigned by the Chief Justice. Such additional circuit judges shall be elected in the same manner and for the same term as provided in the preceding paragraph of this section for other circuit judges, except that residence in a particular county or circuit shall not be a qualification for office.

Section 14. Rotation of Judges

Judges of the Circuit Court shall interchange circuits and all judges shall be systematically rotated throughout the State as directed by the Chief Justice.

Section 15. Qualifications of Justices and Judges

No person shall be eligible to the office of Chief Justice, Associate Justice of the Supreme Court, judge of the court of appeals, or judge of the circuit court who is not at the time of his election a citizen of the United States and of this State, and has not attained the age of at least thirty-two years, has not been a licensed attorney at law for at least eight years, and has not been a resident of this State for five years next preceding his election.

Any justice or judge serving in office on the effective date of the provisions of this section requiring a justice or judge to be at least thirty-two years of age and to have at least eight years of service as a licensed attorney at law who is not of that age or who has not been licensed for this required period of time may continue to serve for the remainder of his current term and is considered to have the requisite age and years of service as a licensed attorney for purposes of future re-elections to that judicial office.

Section 16. Compensation of Justices and Judges; Practice of Law and Dual Office Holding

The Justices of the Supreme Court and the judges of the Court of Appeals and Circuit Court shall each receive compensation for their services to be fixed by law, which shall not be diminished during the term. They shall not, while in office, engage in the practice of law, hold office in a political party, or hold any other office or position of profit under the United States, the State, or its political subdivisions except in the militia, nor shall they be allowed any fees or perquisites of office. Any such Justice or judge who shall become a candidate for a popularly elected office shall thereby forfeit his judicial office.

Section 17. Removal or Retirement of Judges

Within the unified court system, the Supreme Court shall have power, after hearing, to remove or retire any judge from office upon a finding of disability seriously interfering with the performance of his duties which is, or is likely to become, of a permanent character. A Justice shall not sit in any hearing involving his own removal or retirement. Implementation and enforcement of this section may be by rule or order of the Supreme Court.

Section 18. Vacancies

All vacancies in the Supreme Court, Court of Appeals, or Circuit Court shall be filled by elections as prescribed in Sections 3, 8, and 13 of this article; provided, that if the unexpired term does not exceed one year such vacancy may be filled by the Governor. When a vacancy is filled by either appointment or election, the incumbent shall hold office only for the unexpired term of his predecessor.

Section 19. Disqualification of Justices and judges; Temporary Appointments

The General Assembly shall specify the grounds for disqualification of Justices and judges to sit on certain cases. The General Assembly shall also provide for the temporary appointment of men learned in the law to sit as special Justices and judges when the necessity for such appointment shall arise.

Section 20. Powers of Justices and Judges at Chambers

Each of the Justices of the Supreme Court and judges of the Court of Appeals and Circuit Court and of all other courts of record shall have the same power at chambers to issue writs of habeas corpus, mandamus, quo warranto, certiorari, prohibition, and interlocutory writs or orders of injunction as when in open court. The judges of the Court of Appeals and Circuit Court and other courts of record shall have such additional powers at chambers as the General Assembly may provide, except in matters required to be determined in a public trial.

Section 21. Charge to Jury

Judges shall not charge juries in respect to matters of fact, but shall declare the law.

Section 22. Grand and Petit Juries

The petit jury of the Circuit Court shall consist of twelve members and the number of jurors of other courts must be determined by law. All jurors in any trial court must agree to a verdict in order to render the same. The grand jury of each county, and the state grand jury, as the General Assembly may establish by general law, shall consist of eighteen members, twelve of whom must agree in a matter before it can be submitted to the Court. Each juror must be a resident of this State and have such other qualifications as the General Assembly may prescribe.

Section 23. Change of Venue

It shall be the duty of the General Assembly to pass laws for the change of venue in all cases, civil and criminal, upon proper showing, supported by affidavit, that a fair and impartial trial cannot be had in the county where such action or prosecution was commenced. The State shall have the same right to move for a change of venue that a defendant has for such offenses as the General Assembly may prescribe.

Section 24. Law Enforcement Officials, Prosecutors and Administrative Officers; Attorney General

There shall be elected in each county by the electors thereof a clerk of the circuit court, a sheriff, and a coroner; and in each judicial circuit a solicitor shall be elected by the electors thereof. All of these officers shall serve for terms of four years and until their successors are elected and qualify. The General Assembly shall provide by law for their duties and compensation.
The General Assembly also may provide by law for the age and qualifications of sheriffs and coroners, and the selection, duties, and compensation of other appropriate officials to enforce the criminal laws of the State, to prosecute persons under these laws, and to carry on the administrative functions of the courts of the State.

The Attorney General shall be the chief prosecuting officer of the State with authority to supervise the prosecution of all criminal cases in courts of record.

Section 25. Publication of Supreme Court and Court of Appeals Decisions

The General Assembly shall provide for the publication of the decisions of the Supreme Court and the Court of Appeals.

Section 26. Magistrates

The Governor, by and with the advice and consent of the Senate, shall appoint a number of magistrates for each county as provided by law. The General Assembly shall provide for their terms of office and their civil and criminal jurisdiction. The terms of office must be uniform throughout the State.

Section 27. Judicial Merit Selection Commission

In addition to the qualifications for circuit court and court of appeals judges and Supreme Court justices contained in this article, the General Assembly by law shall establish a Judicial Merit Selection Commission to consider the qualifications and fitness of candidates for all judicial positions on these courts and on other courts of this State which are filled by election of the General Assembly. The General Assembly must elect the judges and justices from among the nominees of the commission to fill a vacancy on these courts.

No person may be elected to these judicial positions unless he or she has been found qualified by the commission. Before a sitting member of the General Assembly may submit an application with the commission for his nomination to a judicial office, and before the commission may accept or consider such an application, the member of the General Assembly must first resign his office and have been out of office for a period established by law. Before a member of the commission may submit an application with the commission for his nomination to a judicial office, and before the commission may accept or consider such an application, the member of the commission must not have been a member of the commission for a period to be established by law.

ARTICLE VI: OFFICERS

Section 1. Eligibility for Office; Terms

No person may be popularly elected to and serve in any office in this State or its political subdivisions unless he possesses the qualifications of an elector, is not disqualified by age as prescribed in this Constitution, and has not been convicted of a felony under state or federal law or convicted of tampering with a voting machine, fraudulent registration or voting, bribery at elections, procuring or offering to procure votes by bribery, voting more than once at elections, impersonating a voter, or swearing falsely at elections/taking oath in another's name, or has not pled guilty or nolo contendere to these offenses. However, notwithstanding any other provision of this Constitution, this prohibition does not apply to a person who has been pardoned under state or federal law or to a person who files for public of fice fifteen years or more after the completion date of service of the sentence, including probation and parole time, nor shall any person, serving in office prior to the ratification of this provision, be required to vacate the office to which he is elected. No person may be elected or appointed to office in this State for life or during good behavior, but the terms of all officers must be for some specified period except officers in the militia.

Section 2. Person Denying Existence of Supreme Being Not to Hold Office

No person who denies the existence of the Supreme Being shall hold any office under this Constitution.

Section 3. Dual Office Holding

No person may hold two offices of honor or profit at the same time. This limitation does not apply to officers in the militia, notaries public, members of lawfully and regularly organized fire departments, constables, or delegates to a constitutional convention.

Section 4. Officers to Take and Subscribe Oath

The Governor, Lieutenant Governor, and all other officers of the State and its political subdivisions, before entering upon the duties of their respective offices, shall take and subscribe the oath of office as prescribed in Section 5 of this article.

Section 5. Form of Oath

Members of the General Assembly, and all officers, before they enter upon the duties of their respective offices, and all members of the bar, before they enter upon the practice of their profession, shall take and subscribe the following oath: "I do solemnly swear (or affirm) that I am duly qualified, according to the Constitution of this State, to exercise the duties of the office to which I have been elected, (or appointed), and that I will, to the best of my ability, discharge the duties thereof, and preserve, protect, and defend the Constitution of this State and of the United States. So help me God."

Section 6. Commissions; Great Seal

The Governor shall commission all officers of the State. All commissions shall be issued in the name and by the authority of the State of South Carolina, sealed with the Great Seal, signed by the Governor, and countersigned by the Secretary of State. The seal of the State now in use shall be used by the Governor officially, and shall be called "The Great Seal of the State of South Carolina."

Section 7. Elective Offices; Terms; Duties; Compensation

There shall be elected by the qualified voters of the State a Secretary of State, an Attorney General, a Treasurer, a Superintendent of Education, Comptroller General, Commissioner of Agriculture, and an Adjutant General who shall hold their respective offices for a term of four years, coterminous with that of the Governor. The duties and compensation of such offices shall be prescribed by law and their compensation shall be neither increased nor diminished during the period for which they shall have been elected.

Beginning upon the expiration of the term of the Adjutant General serving in office on the date of the ratification of the provisions of this paragraph, the Adjutant General must be appointed by the Governor, upon the advice and consent of the Senate. The appointed Adjutant General shall serve for a term not coterminous with the Governor and may be removed only for cause. The General Assembly shall provide by law for the term, duties, compensation, and qualifications for office, the procedures by which the appointment is made, and the procedures by which the Adjutant General may be removed from office

Section 8. Suspension and Prosecution of Officers Accused of Crime

Whenever it appears to the satisfaction of the Governor that probable cause exists to charge any officer of the State or its political subdivisions who has the custody of public or trust funds with embezzlement or the appropriation of public or trust funds to private use, then the Governor shall direct his immediate prosecution by the proper officer, and upon indictment by a grand jury or, upon the waiver of such indictment if permitted by law, the Governor shall suspend such officer and appoint one in his stead, until he shall have been acquitted. In case of conviction, the position shall be declared vacant and the vacancy filled as may be provided by law.

Any officer of the State or its political subdivisions, except members and officers of the Legislative and Judicial Branches, who has been indicted by a grand jury for a crime involving moral turpitude or who has waived such indictment if permitted by law may be suspended by the Governor until he shall have been acquitted. In case of conviction the office shall be declared vacant and the vacancy filled as may be provided by law.

Section 9. Removal of Officers

Officers shall be removed for incapacity, misconduct, or neglect of duty, in such manner as may be provided by law when no mode of trial or removal is provided in this Constitution.

ARTICLE VII: COUNTIES AND COUNTY GOVERNMENT

Section 1. Formation of New Counties; County Seats and Names

The General Assembly may establish new Counties in the following manner: Whenever one-third of the qualified electors within the area of each section of an old County proposed to be cut off to form a new County shall petition the Governor for the creation of a new County, setting forth the boundaries and showing compliance with the requirements of this Article, the Governor shall order an election, within a reasonable time thereafter, by the qualified electors within the proposed area, in which election they shall vote "Yes" or "No" upon the question of creating said new County; and at the same election the question of a name and a County seat for such County shall be submitted to the electors.

Section 2. Section of Old County to Be Cut Off

If two-thirds of the qualified electors voting at such election shall vote "Yes" upon such questions, then the General Assembly at the next session shall establish such new County: Provided, No section of the County proposed to be dismembered shall be thus cut off without consent by a two-thirds vote of those voting in such section; and no County shall be formed without complying with all the conditions imposed in this Article. An election upon the question of forming the same proposed new County shall not be held oftener than once in four years.

Section 3. Inhabitants; Taxable Property; Area of New County

No new County hereafter formed shall contain less than one one-hundred and twenty-fourth part of the whole number of inhabitants of the State, nor shall it have less assessed taxable property than one and one half million of dollars as shown by the last tax returns, nor shall it contain less area than four hundred square miles.

Section 4. Area, Taxable Property, and Inhabitants of Old County

No old County shall be reduced to less area than five hundred square miles, to less assessed taxable property than two million dollars, nor to a smaller population than fifteen thousand inhabitants.

Section 5. Eight-Mile Limit

In the formation of new Counties no old County shall be cut within eight miles of its courthouse building.

Section 6. Indebtedness

All new Counties hereafter formed shall bear a just apportionment of the valid indebtedness of the old County or Counties from which they have been formed.

Section 7. Alteration of County Lines

The General Assembly shall have the power to alter County lines at any time: Provided, That before any existing County line is altered the question shall be first submitted to the qualified electors of the territory proposed to be taken from one County and given to another, and shall have received two-thirds of the votes cast: Provided, further, That the change shall not reduce the County from which the territory is taken below the limits prescribed in Sections 3, 4 and 5 of this Article: Provided, That the proper proportion of the existing County indebtedness of the section so transferred shall be assumed by the County to which the territory is transferred.

Section 8. Removal of County Seat

No County Seat shall be removed except by a vote of two-thirds of the qualified electors of said County voting in an election held for that purpose, but such election shall not be held in any

County oftener than once in five years.

Section 9. Election District; Body Corporate

Each County shall constitute one election district, and shall be a body politic and corporate.

Section 10. Consolidation of Two or More Counties

The General Assembly may provide for the consolidation of two or more existing Counties if a majority of the qualified electors of such Counties voting at an election held for that purpose shall vote separately therefore, but such election shall not be held oftener than once in four years in the same Counties.

Section 11. Townships; Body Corporate; Township and County Government

Each of the several townships of this State, with names and boundaries as now established by law, shall constitute a body politic and corporate, but this shall not prevent the General Assembly from organizing other townships or changing the boundaries of those already established; and the General Assembly may provide such system of township government as it shall think proper in any and all the Counties, and may make special provisions for municipal government and for the protection of chartered rights and powers of municipalities: Provided, That this Section shall not apply to the following townships in the following Counties: Dunklin and Oaklawn in the County of Greenville; the Townships of Cokesbury, Ninety Six and Cooper, in the County of Greenwood; Sullivan Township, in the County of Laurens; Huiett and Pine Grove, in the County of Saluda. That the corporate existence of said townships be, and the same is hereby, destroyed, and all officers under said townships are abolished, and all corporate agents removed.

Section 12. Boundaries of Counties; Boundaries of Saluda and Edgefield

Until changed by the General Assembly, as allowed by this Constitution, the boundaries of the several counties shall remain as now established, except that the boundaries of the County of Edgefield shall undergo such changes as are made necessary by the formation of a new County from a portion of Edgefield, to be known as Saluda, the boundaries of which are set forth in a Constitutional Ordinance. The election ordered in said ordinance for the location of its County seat shall be held under the Constitution and laws now of force. And the General Assembly shall provide for the assessment of property in the County of Saluda for the fiscal year beginning January first, eighteen hundred and ninety-six, and for the collection of said taxes when assessed.

Section 13. Judicial and Congressional Districts; Voting Precincts

The General Assembly may at any time arrange the various Counties into Judicial Circuits, and into Congressional Districts, including the County of Saluda, as it may deem wise and proper, and may establish or alter the location of voting precincts in any County.

Section 14. No County Line through City or Town

Hereafter no County lines shall be so established as to pass through any incorporated city or town of this State.

Section 15. Regional Councils of Government

The General Assembly may authorize the governing body of a county or municipality, in combination with other counties and municipalities, to create, participate in, and provide financial support for organizations to study and make recommendations on matters affecting the public health, safety, general welfare, education, recreation, pollution control, utilities, planning, development and such other matters as the common interest of the participating governments may dictate. Such organizations, which shall be designated regional councils of government, may include political subdivisions of other states. The studies and recommendations by such organizations shall be made on behalf of and directed to the participating governments and other governmental instrumentalities which operate programs within the jurisdiction of the participating governments.

The legislature may authorize participating governments to provide financial support for facilities and services required to implement recommendations of such organizations which are accepted and approved by the governing bodies of the participating political subdivisions. Such organizations shall not have the power to levy taxes. Local funds for the support of such organizations shall consist of contributions from the participating political subdivisions as may be authorized and granted by their respective governing bodies. The prohibitions against dual office holding contained in Section 2 of Article 2 and Section 24 of Article 3 of this Constitution shall not apply to any elected or appointed official or employee of government who serves as a member of a regional council.

ARTICLE VIII: LOCAL GOVERNMENT

Section 1. Powers of Political Subdivisions Continued

The powers possessed by all counties, cities, towns, and other political subdivisions at the effective date of this Constitution shall continue until changed in a manner provided by law.

Section 2. Boundaries of Counties

Until changed by the General Assembly, as allowed by this Constitution, the boundaries of the several counties shall remain as now established.

Section 3. Number of Counties

No more than forty-six counties shall exist at any time, but the General Assembly may provide for a lesser number.

Section 4. Merger of Counties

The General Assembly shall provide by law for the merger of adjoining counties. Such mergers shall be permitted by the General Assembly only upon the request of the governing bodies of the counties or upon petition by ten percent of the registered voters in each of the counties involved. No merger shall take place unless a majority of the electors voting on the question shall vote therefore in each of the counties.

Section 5. Merger of Parts of Counties with Adjoining Counties

The General Assembly shall provide for the merger of a part or parts of a county with one or more adjoining counties upon request by the governing body of the county in which such part or parts are located, or upon petition by ten percent of the registered voters in the area desiring to transfer to another county. No merger shall take place unless two thirds of the qualified electors voting on the question in the territory to be transferred and a majority of the electors voting on the question in the county to which the territory is proposed to be annexed shall vote therefore.

Section 6. Removal of County Seat

No county seat shall be removed except by a vote of two thirds of the qualified electors of the county voting in an election held for that purpose; nor shall any county seat be established unless a majority of the electors voting on the question shall vote therefore.

Section 7. Organization, Power, and Duties of Counties; Special Laws Prohibited

The General Assembly shall provide by general law for the structure, organization, powers, duties, functions, and the responsibilities of counties, including the power to tax different areas at different rates of taxation related to the nature and level of governmental services provided. Alternate forms of government, not to exceed five, shall be established. No laws for a specific county shall be enacted and no county shall be exempted from the general laws or laws applicable to the selected alternative form of government.

Section 8. Incorporation of New Municipalities; Readjustment of Municipal Boundaries; Merger of Municipalities; Special Laws Prohibited

The General Assembly shall provide by general law the criteria and the procedures for the incorporation of new municipalities and for the readjustment of municipal boundaries and for the merger of incorporated municipalities provided that any city or town shall be organized with the consent of a majority of the electors voting in such election who reside in and are entitled by law to vote within the district proposed to be incorporated. No local or special laws shall be enacted for these purposes; provided, that the General Assembly may vary such provisions among the alternative forms of government.

Section 9. Organization, Powers, and Duties of Municipalities

The structure and organization, powers, duties, functions, and responsibilities of the municipalities shall be established by general law; provided, that not more than five alternative forms of government shall be authorized.

Section 10. Law or Exemption for a Specific Municipality Prohibited

No laws for a specific municipality shall be enacted, and no municipality shall be exempted from the laws applicable to municipalities or applicable to a particular form of government selected by any municipality as authorized by Section 9 of this article.

Section 11. Adoption and Amendment of Municipal Charters

The General Assembly shall provide by general law two or more optional procedures by which incorporated municipalities may select a charter commission for the framing, publishing, and adopting of a municipal charter and the making of amendments thereto. Any municipality so eligible shall have the power to frame and to amend a municipal charter setting forth its governmental structure and organization, powers, duties, functions, and responsibilities. No municipal charter so framed shall contain any provision inconsistent with this Constitution or the general law provisions enacted pursuant to Section 14 of this article. Such charter or charters or charter amendments shall not become effective until approved by a majority of the qualified electors of the municipality voting thereon. The General Assembly may determine the classes of municipalities to which the provisions of this section apply.

Section 12. Consolidation of Counties with Municipalities and Other Political Subdivisions

Notwithstanding any other provisions of this Constitution, any county may consolidate with the municipalities and other political subdivisions within its limits into a single unit of government, which shall be known as a consolidated political subdivision. The General Assembly shall provide by law for a referendum on such consolidations and for procedures for the framing of a charter for the new political subdivision. Such referendum shall be held only upon the request of the governing body of the county or upon petition of ten percent of the registered electors within the county.

Such consolidation shall not take place unless approved by a majority of the qualified electors voting on the questions of the consolidation and on the charter therefore in the same election or in successive elections held for these purposes. All municipalities and all other political subdivisions within the county not continued by the approved charter shall cease to exist at the effective date of the consolidation.

Any political subdivision created by such a consolidation shall have the power to frame, to publish, to adopt, and to amend a charter setting forth its governmental structure and organization, powers, duties, functions, and responsibilities. No charter so framed shall contain any provision inconsistent with this Constitution or with general law provisions applicable in all municipalities or counties enacted pursuant to Section 14 of this article.

Such charter or charter amendments shall not become effective until approved by a majority of the qualified electors of such political subdivisions voting on the question.

Section 13. Joint Administration of Functions and Exercise of Powers

(A) Any county, incorporated municipality, or other political subdivision may agree with the State or with any other political subdivision for the joint administration of any function and exercise of powers and the sharing of the costs thereof.

(B) Nothing in this Constitution may be construed to prohibit the State or any of its counties, incorporated municipalities, or other political subdivisions from agreeing to share the lawful cost, responsibility, and administration of functions with any one or more governments, whether within or without this State.

(C) The prohibitions against dual officeholding contained in Article VI of this Constitution do not apply to any elected or appointed official or employee who serves on a regional council of government created under the authority of this section.

(D) Counties may jointly develop an industrial or business park with other counties within the geographical boundaries of one or more of the member counties. The area comprising the parks and all property having a situs therein is exempt from all ad valorem taxation. The owners or lessees of any property situated in the park shall pay an amount equivalent to the property taxes or other in-lieu-of payments that would have been due and payable except for the exemption herein provided. The participating counties shall reduce the agreement to develop and share expenses and revenues of the park to a written instrument which is binding on all participating counties. Included within expenses are the costs to provide public services such as sewage, water, fire, and police protection. Notwithstanding the above provisions of this subsection, before a group of member counties may establish an industrial or business park as authorized herein, the General Assembly must first provide by law for the manner in which the value of the property in the park will be considered for purposes of bonded indebtedness of political subdivisions and school districts and for purposes of computing the index of taxpaying ability pursuant to any provision of law which measures the relative fiscal capacity of a school district to support its schools based on the assessed valuation of taxable property in the district as compared to the assessed valuation of the taxable property in all school districts of this State.

Section 14. General Law Provisions Not to Be Set Aside
In enacting provisions required or authorized by this article, general law provisions applicable to the following matters shall not be set aside:

(1) The freedoms guaranteed every person;

(2) election and suffrage qualifications;

(3) bonded indebtedness of governmental units;

(4) the structure for and the administration of the State's judicial system;

(5) criminal laws and the penalties and sanctions for the transgression thereof; and

(6) the structure and the administration of any governmental service or function, responsibility for which rests with the State government or which requires statewide uniformity.

Section 15. Consent of Local Governing Body to Certain Laws Required

No law shall be passed by the General Assembly granting the right to construct and operate in a public street or on public property a street or other railway, telegraph, telephone or electric plant, or to erect water, sewer or gas works for public use, or to lay mains for any purpose, or to use the streets for any other such facility, without first obtaining the consent of the governing body of the municipality in control of the streets or public places proposed to be occupied for any such or like purpose; nor shall any law be passed by the General Assembly granting the right to construct and operate in a public street or on public property a street or other railway, or to erect waterworks for public use, or to lay water or sewer mains for any purpose, or to use the streets for any facility other than telephone, telegraph, gas and electric, without first obtaining the consent of the governing body of the county or the consolidated political subdivision in control of the streets or public places proposed to be occupied for any such or like purpose.

Section 16. Acquisition and Operation of Public Utility Systems

Any incorporated municipality may, upon a majority vote of the electors of such political subdivision who shall vote on the question, acquire by initial construction or purchase and may operate gas, water, sewer, electric, transportation or other public utility systems and plants.

Any county or consolidated political subdivision created under this Constitution may, upon a majority vote of the electors voting on the question in such county or consolidated political subdivision, acquire by initial construction or purchase and may operate water, sewer, transportation or other public utility systems and plants other than gas and electric; provided this provision shall not prohibit the continued operation of gas and electric, water, sewer or other such utility systems of a municipality which becomes a part of a consolidated political subdivision.

Section 17. Construction of Constitution and Laws

The provisions of this Constitution and all laws concerning local government shall be liberally construed in their favor. Powers, duties, and responsibilities granted local government subdivisions by this Constitution and by law shall include those fairly implied and not prohibited by this Constitution.

Section 18. Assignment and Regulation of Territories for Electrical and Gas Utilities

Sections 15 and 16 of this article notwithstanding, the General Assembly shall provide by general law for the assignment and regulation of territories for electrical and gas utilities within consolidated political subdivisions, except within former municipal corporate limits as they existed on the date of consolidation whenever such municipality owns and operates its own electric or gas system.

ARTICLE VIII-A: ALCOHOLIC LIQUORS AND BEVERAGES

Section 1. Powers of General Assembly

In the exercise of the police power the General Assembly has the right to prohibit and to regulate the manufacture, sale, and retail of alcoholic liquors or beverages within the State. The General Assembly may license persons or corporations to manufacture, sell, and retail alcoholic liquors or beverages within the State under the rules and restrictions as it considers proper, including the right to sell alcoholic liquors or beverages in containers of such size as the General Assembly considers appropriate. The General Assembly may prohibit the manufacture, sale, and retail of alcoholic liquors and beverages within the State, and may authorize and empower state, county, and municipal officers, all or either, under the authority and in the name of the State, to buy in any market and retail within the State liquors and beverages in such packages and quantities, under such rules and regulations, as it considers expedient. However, a license must not be granted to sell alcoholic beverages in less quantities than one ounce in licensed retail stores, or to sell them between seven o'clock p.m. and nine o'clock a.m., or to sell them to be drunk on the premises; however, the General Assembly shall not delegate to any municipal corporation the power to issue licenses to sell alcoholic liquors or beverages. However, licenses may be granted to sell and consume alcoholic liquors and beverages on the premises of businesses which engage primarily and substantially in the preparation and serving of meals or furnishing of lodging or on the premises of certain nonprofit organizations with limited membership not open to the general public, during such hours as the General Assembly may provide.

ARTICLE IX: CORPORATIONS

Section 1. Regulation of Common Carriers, Publicly-Owned

Utilities and Privately-Owned Utilities Serving the Public
The General Assembly shall provide for appropriate regulation of common carriers, publicly owned utilities, and privately owned utilities serving the public as and to the extent required by the public interest.

Section 2. Formation, Organization, and Regulation of Corporations

The General Assembly shall provide by general law for the formation, organization, and regulation of corporations and shall prescribe their powers, rights, duties, and liabilities, including the powers, rights, duties, and liabilities of their officers and stockholders or members.

ARTICLE X: FINANCE, TAXATION, AND BONDED DEBT

Section 1. Taxation and Assessment

The General Assembly may provide for the ad valorem taxation by the State or any of its subdivisions of all real and personal property. The assessment of all property shall be equal and uniform in the following classifications:

(1) All real and personal property owned by or leased to manufacturers, utilities and mining operations and used by the manufacturer, utility or mining operation, in the conduct of such business shall be taxed on an assessment equal to ten and one-half percent of the fair market value of such property.

(2) All real and personal property owned by or leased to companies primarily engaged in transportation for hire of persons or property and used by the company in the conduct of such business shall be taxed on an assessment equal to nine and one-half percent of the fair market value of such property.

(3) The legal residence and not more than five acres contiguous thereto shall be taxed on an assessment equal to four percent of the fair market value of such property.

(4) Agricultural real property which is actually used for such purposes shall be taxed on an assessment equal to:

(A) four percent of its value for such purposes when owned or leased to individuals or partnerships and certain corporations which do not:

(i) have more than ten shareholders;

(ii) have as a shareholder a person (other than an estate) who is not an individual;

(iii) have a nonresident alien as a shareholder; and

(iv) have more than one class of stock.

(B) six percent of its value for such purposes when owned or leased to corporations, except for certain corporations specified in (A) above. Provided, that the General Assembly shall by general law provide for a penalty system on lands classified as agricultural lands to insure the proper utilization of this classification.

(5) All other real property not herein provided for shall be taxed on an assessment equal to six percent of the fair market value of such property.

(6) All inventories of business establishments shall be taxed on an assessment equal to six percent of the fair market value of such property.

(7) All farm machinery and equipment except motor vehicles licensed for use on the highways owned by farmers and used on agricultural lands shall be taxed on an assessment equal to five percent of the fair market value.

(8)(A) Except as provided in subitem (B) of this item, all other personal property must be taxed on an assessment equal to ten and one-half percent of the fair market value of the property.

(B)(1) Personal motor vehicles which must be titled by a state or federal agency, limited to passenger motor vehicles and pickup trucks, as defined by law, must be taxed on an assessment equal to the following percentage of fair market value of the property: Property Tax Year Percentage

year 1: 9.75

year 2: 9.00

year 3: 8.25

year 4: 7.50

year 5: 6.75

year: 6

and after: 6.00

(2) This subitem applies for property tax years beginning after 2001 or for earlier tax years as the General Assembly may provide by law.

Section 2. Defining Classes of Property and Values for Property Tax Purposes; Transition to Assessment Ratios; Continuance of Existing Statutes Pertaining to Assessment Methods; Changing Assessment Ratios

(a) The General Assembly may define the classes of property and values for property tax purposes of the classes of property set forth in Section 1 of this article and establish administrative procedures for property owners to qualify for a particular classification.

(b) The General Assembly may provide for a gradual transition to any ratio as set out in Section 1 over a period not to exceed seven years.

(c) Statutes pertaining to the methods of assessment of property for ad valorem taxation not in conflict with this article shall continue in force until changed by an act of the General Assembly.

(d) The General Assembly may change the ratios as set forth in Section 1, but only with the approval of at least two-thirds of the membership of each house.

Section 3. Property Exempt from Ad Valorem Taxation

There shall be exempt from ad valorem taxation:

(a) all property of the State, counties, municipalities, school districts and other political subdivisions, if the property is used exclusively for public purposes;

(b) all property of all schools, colleges and other institutions of learning and all charitable institutions in the nature of hospitals and institutions caring for the infirmed, the handicapped, the aged, children and indigent persons, except where the profits of such institutions are applied to private use;

(c) all property of all public libraries, churches, parsonages and burying grounds;

(d) all property of all charitable trusts and foundations used exclusively for charitable and public purposes;

(e) all household goods and furniture used in the home of the owner of such goods and furniture, but this exemption shall not apply to household goods used in hotels, rooming houses, apartments or other places of business;

(f) all inventories of manufactures, except manufactured articles which have been offered for sale at retail or which have been available for sale at retail;

(g) all new manufacturing establishments located in any of the counties of this State after July 1, 1977, for five years from the time of establishment and all additions to the existing manufacturing establishments located in any of the counties of this State for five years from the time each of these additions is made if the cost of the addition is fifty thousand dollars or more. The additions shall include additional machinery and equipment installed in the plant. The exemptions authorized in this item for manufacturing establishments, and additions to those manufacturing establishments, do not include exemptions from school taxes or municipal taxes but include only county taxes. All manufacturing establishments and all additions to existing manufacturing establishments exempt under existing statutes are allowed their exemptions provided for by statute until the exemptions expire. Municipal governing bodies may by ordinance exempt from municipal ad valorem taxation for not more than five years all new manufacturing establishments located in any of the municipalities of this State after July 1, 1985, and all additions to the existing manufacturing establishments, including additional machinery and equipment, located in any of the municipalities of this State costing fifty thousand dollars or more made after July 1, 1985. Exemptions from municipal taxation granted pursuant to this item may not result in any refund of taxes;

The governing body of a municipality may by ordinance exempt from municipal ad valorem taxation for not more than five years:

(1) all new corporate headquarters, corporate office facilities, distribution facilities located in the municipality, and additions to such facilities; and

(2) all facilities of new enterprises engaged in research and development activities located in the municipality, and additions to such facilities.
The exemptions allowed pursuant to this paragraph are subject to those terms and conditions that the General Assembly may provide by law.

(h) all facilities or equipment of industrial plants which are designed for the elimination, mitigation, prevention, treatment, abatement or control of water, air or noise pollution;

(i) a homestead exemption for persons sixty-five years of age and older, for persons permanently and totally disabled and for blind persons in the amount of ten thousand dollars of the fair market value of the homestead under conditions prescribed by the General Assembly by general law; provided, that the amount may be increased by the General Assembly by general law, passed by a majority vote of both houses;

(j) intangible personal property.
The exemptions provided in subitems (c) and (d) for real property shall not extend beyond the buildings and premises actually occupied by the owners of such real property. Homestead exemptions from ad valorem taxation not specifically provided for in this section may be provided for by the General Assembly by general law. In addition to the exemptions listed in this section, the General Assembly may provide for exemptions from the property tax, by general laws applicable uniformly to property throughout the State and in all political subdivisions, but only with the approval of two-thirds of the members of each House. All exemptions not specifically provided for or authorized in this article shall be repealed March 1, 1978. The General Assembly shall provide for methods and procedures in applying for the exemption of any property as is described in this section. In addition to the exemptions provided and authorized in this section, subject to statutory authorization, the governing body of a county by ordinance may impose a sales and use tax in order to exempt all or a portion of the value of private passenger motor vehicles, motorcycles, general aviation aircraft, boats, and boat motors from property taxes levied in the county. This exemption, or its subsequent rescission, is allowed only pursuant to a referendum held in the county in the manner that the General Assembly provides by law.

Section 4. One Assessment for All Taxes

The General Assembly shall provide for the assessment of all property for taxation, whether for state, county, school, municipal or any other political subdivision. All taxes shall be levied on that assessment.

Section 5. No Tax without Consent; Taxes to Be Levied in Pursuance of Law

No tax, subsidy or charge shall be established, fixed, laid or levied, under any pretext whatsoever, without the consent of the people or their representatives lawfully assembled. Any tax which shall be levied shall distinctly state the public purpose to which the proceeds of the tax shall be applied.

Section 6. Establishment of Method of Valuation for Assessment of Real Property within State

Except as otherwise provided in this section, the General Assembly may vest the power of assessing and collecting taxes in all of the political subdivisions of the State, including counties, municipalities, special purpose districts, public service districts, and school districts. Property tax levies shall be uniform in respect to persons and property within the jurisdiction of the body imposing such taxes; provided, that on properties located in an area receiving special benefits from the taxes collected, special levies may be permitted by general law applicable to the same type of political subdivision throughout the State, and the General Assembly shall specify the precise condition under which such special levies shall be assessed. For the tax year beginning 2007, each parcel of real property in this State shall have a maximum value for ad valorem taxes that does not exceed its fair market value. The General Assembly is authorized, by general law, to define "fair market value" and to define when property has been improved or when losses have occurred to change the value of the real property.

The General Assembly shall establish, through the enactment of general law, and not through the enactment of local legislation pertaining to a single county or other political subdivision, the method of assessment of real property within the State that shall apply to each political subdivision within the State. Each political subdivision shall value real property by a method in which the value of each parcel of real property, adjusted for improvements and losses, does not increase more than fifteen percent every five years unless, as defined by the General Assembly, an assessable transfer of interest occurs.

Notwithstanding any other provision of law, for the purposes of calculating the limit on bonded indebtedness of political subdivisions and school districts, pursuant to Sections 14 and 15 of Article X, respectively of the Constitution of this State, the assessed values of all taxable property within a political subdivision or school district shall not be lower than the assessed values of tax year 2006.

Whenever there is a merger of governments authorized under Section 12 of Article VIII, tax districts may be created, based upon the services rendered in each district, but tax levies must be uniform in respect to persons and property within each such district.

Section 7. Limitation on Annual Expenditures of State Government and Number of State Employees; Annual Budgets and Expenses of Political Subdivisions and School Districts

(a) The General Assembly shall provide by law for a budget process to insure that annual expenditures of state government may not exceed annual state revenue.

(b) Each political subdivision of the State as defined in Section 14 of this article and each school district of this State shall prepare and maintain annual budgets which provide for sufficient income to meet its estimated expenses for each year. Whenever it shall happen that the ordinary expenses of a political subdivision for any year shall exceed the income of such political subdivision, the governing body of such political subdivision shall provide for levying a tax in the ensuing year sufficient, with other sources of income, to pay the deficiency of the preceding year together with the estimated expenses for such ensuing year. The General Assembly shall establish procedures to insure that the provisions of this section are enforced.

(c) The General Assembly shall prescribe by law a spending limitation on appropriations for the operation of state government which shall provide that annual increases in such appropriations may not exceed the average growth rate of the economy of the State as measured by a process provided for by the law which prescribes the limitations on appropriations; provided, however, the limitation may be suspended for any one fiscal year by a special vote as provided in this subsection. During the regular session of the General Assembly in 1990 and during every fifth annual regular session thereafter, the General Assembly shall conduct and complete a review of the law implementing this subsection. During such session, only a vote of two-thirds of the members of each branch present and voting shall be required to change the existing limitation on appropriation. Unless that is done, the existing limitations shall remain unchanged.

Upon implementation of the provisions of this subsection by law, such law may not be amended or repealed except by the special vote as provided in this subsection.

The special vote referred to in this subsection means an affirmative vote in each branch of the General Assembly by two-thirds of the members present and voting, but not less than three-fifths of the total membership in each branch.

(d) The General Assembly shall prescribe by law a limitation on the number of state employees which shall provide that the annual increase in such number may not exceed the average growth rate in the population of the State measured by a process provided for in the law which prescribes that employment limitation; provided, however, the limitation may be suspended for any one fiscal year by a special vote as provided in this subsection.

Upon implementation of the provisions of this subsection by law, such law may not be amended or repealed except by the special vote provided in this subsection.

The special vote referred to in this subsection means an affirmative vote in each branch of the General Assembly by two-thirds of the members present and voting, but not less than three-fifths of the total membership in each branch.

Section 8. Payments from Treasuries

Money shall be drawn from the treasury of the State or the treasury of any of its political subdivisions only in pursuance of appropriations made by law.

Section 9. Statement of Receipts and Expenditures
An accurate statement of the receipts and expenditures of the public money shall be published annually in such manner as may be prescribed by law.

Section 10. Claims Against State

The General Assembly may direct, by law, in what manner claims against the State may be established and adjusted.

Section 11. Credit of State and Political Subdivisions

The credit of neither the State nor of any of its political subdivisions shall be pledged or loaned for the benefit of any individual, company, association, corporation, or any religious or other private education institution except as permitted by Section 3, Article XI of this Constitution. Neither the State nor any of its political subdivisions shall become a joint owner of or stockholder in any company, association, or corporation. The General Assembly may, however, authorize the South Carolina Public Service Authority to become a joint owner with privately owned electric utilities, including electric cooperatives, of electric generation or transmission facilities, or both, and to enter into and carry out agreements with respect to such jointly owned facilities.

Provided, however, the General Assembly may obligate or appropriate state funds in order to participate in federal or federally aided disaster related grant or loan programs for individuals or families, but only to the extent that such state participation is a prerequisite to federal financial assistance. Provided, however, that endowment funds donated specifically to state-supported institutions of higher learning and held by the State Treasurer may be invested and reinvested in equity securities of a corporation within the United States that is registered on a national securities exchange, as provided in the Securities Exchange Act of 1934 or a successor act, or quoted through the National Association of Securities Dealers Automatic Quotations System or similar service. The General Assembly shall implement this paragraph by enacting legislation in which these endowment funds held and invested by the State Treasurer must be invested pursuant to a plan recommended by the State Retirement Systems Investment Panel which must be submitted to and approved by the boards of trustees of the respective colleges and universities.

Notwithstanding any other provision of this section, a municipality, county, special purpose district, or public service district of this State which provides firefighting service and which administers a separate pension plan for its employees performing this service may invest and reinvest the funds in this pension plan in equity securities traded on a national securities exchange as provided in the Securities Exchange Act of 1934 of a successor act, or in equity securities quoted through the National Association of Securities Dealers Automatic Quotations System or similar service.

Section 12. Counties Not to Incur Bonded Indebtedness for Special Services in Certain Areas without Special Tax or Charge on Area or Persons Benefited

No law shall be enacted permitting the incurring of bonded indebtedness by any county for sewage disposal or treatment, fire protection, street lighting, garbage collection and disposal, water service or any other service or facility benefiting only a particular geographical section of the county unless a special assessment, tax or service charge in an amount designed to provide debt service on bonded indebtedness or revenue bonds incurred for such purposes shall be imposed upon the area or persons receiving the benefit therefrom.

Section 13. Bonded Indebtedness of State

(1) Subject to the conditions and limitations in this section, the State shall have power to incur indebtedness in the following categories and in no others: (a) general obligation debt; and (b) indebtedness payable only from a revenue-producing project or from a special source as provided in subsection (9) hereof.

(2) "General obligation debt" shall mean any indebtedness of the State which shall be secured in whole or in part by a pledge of the full faith, credit and taxing power of the State.

(3) General obligation debt may not be incurred except for a public purpose and all general obligation debt shall mature not later than thirty years from the time such indebtedness shall be incurred.

(4) In each act authorizing the incurring of general obligation debt the General Assembly shall allocate on an annual basis sufficient tax revenues to provide for the punctual payment of the principal of and interest on such general obligation debt. If at any time any payment due as the principal of or interest on any general obligation debt shall not be paid as and when the same become due and payable, the State Comptroller General shall forthwith levy and the State Treasurer shall collect an ad valorem tax without limit as to rate or amount upon all taxable property in the State sufficient to meet the payment of the principal and interest of such general obligation debt then due.

(5) If general obligation debt be authorized by (a) two-thirds of the members of each House of the General Assembly; or (b) by a majority vote of the qualified electors of the State voting in a referendum called by the General Assembly there shall be no conditions or restrictions limiting the incurring of such indebtedness except (i) those restrictions and limitations imposed in the authorization to incur such indebtedness, and (ii) the provisions of subsection (3) hereof.

(6) General obligation debt may be also incurred on such terms and conditions as the General Assembly may by law prescribe under the following limitations:

(a) General obligation bonds for highway purposes (highway bonds) may be issued if such bonds shall be additionally secured by a pledge of the revenues derived from the "sources of revenue" as such term is defined in this subsection; provided, that the maximum annual debt service on all highway bonds so additionally secured which shall thereafter be outstanding shall not exceed fifteen percent of the proceeds received from the sources of revenue for the fiscal year next preceding.
For the purpose of this subsection, the term "sources of revenue" shall mean so much of the revenues as may be made applicable by the General Assembly for state highway purposes from any and all taxes or licenses imposed upon individuals or vehicles for the privilege of using the public highways of the State.

(b) General obligation bonds for any state institution of higher learning designated by the General Assembly (state institution bonds) may be issued, if such bonds shall be additionally secured by a pledge of the revenues derived from the tuition fees received by the particular institution of higher learning for which such state institution bonds are issued; provided, that the maximum annual debt service on all state institution bonds so additionally secured issued for such state institution thereafter to be outstanding shall not exceed ninety percent of the sums received by such state institution of higher learning from tuition fees for the fiscal year next preceding.

(c) General obligation bonds for any public purpose including those purposes set forth in (a) and (b) may be issued; provided, that the maximum annual debt service on all general obligation bonds of the State thereafter to be outstanding (excluding highway bonds, state institution bonds, tax anticipation notes, and bond anticipation notes) must not exceed five percent of the general revenues of the State for the fiscal year next preceding (excluding revenues which are authorized to be pledged for state highway bonds and state institution bonds).

Upon implementation of the provisions of this item by law, the percentage rate of general revenues may be reduced to four or increased to seven percent by legislative enactment passed by a two-thirds vote of the total membership of the Senate and a two-thirds vote of the total membership of the House of Representatives.

During the regular session of the General Assembly in 1990 and during every fifth annual regular session thereafter, the General Assembly shall conduct and complete a review of the law implementing this item. Unless during such session that review results in an amendment to or repeal of the law implementing this item, which must be accomplished by legislative enactment passed by a two-thirds vote of the total membership of the Senate and a two-thirds vote of the total membership of the House of Representatives. (1985 Act No. 10, Section 4.)

(7) General obligation indebtedness may be incurred in anticipation of state tax collections (tax anticipation notes) under such terms and conditions as the General Assembly may prescribe by law. Such tax anticipation notes shall be secured by a pledge of such taxes and by a pledge of the full faith, credit and taxing power of the State. All tax anticipation notes shall be expressed to mature not later than ninety days from the end of the fiscal year in which such notes are issued.

(8) General obligation notes may be issued in anticipation of the proceeds of general obligation bonds which may be lawfully issued (bond anticipation notes) under terms and conditions which the General Assembly may prescribe by law. Such bond anticipation notes shall be secured by a pledge of the proceeds of the bonds in anticipation of which such bond anticipation notes are issued and by a pledge of the full faith, credit and taxing power of the State.

Bond anticipation notes shall be expressed to mature not later than one year following the date of issuance, but if the General Assembly shall so authorize by law, bond anticipation notes may be refunded or renewed.

(9) The General Assembly may authorize the State or any of its agencies, authorities or institutions to incur indebtedness for any public purpose payable solely from a revenue-producing project or from a special source, which source does not involve revenues from any tax but may include fees paid for the use of any toll bridge, toll road or tunnel. Such indebtedness may be incurred upon such terms and conditions as the General Assembly may prescribe by law. All indebtedness incurred pursuant to the provisions of this subsection shall contain a statement on the face thereof specifying the sources from which payment is to be made.

Section 14. Bonded Indebtedness of Political Subdivisions

(1) For the purposes of this section, the term "political subdivisions" shall mean the counties of the State, the incorporated municipalities of the State, and special purpose districts, including special purpose districts which are located in more than one county or which are comprised of one or more counties. The term does not include regional planning agencies which are expressly forbidden to incur general obligation debt.

(2) The political subdivisions of the State shall have the power to incur bonded indebtedness in such manner and upon such terms and conditions as the General Assembly shall prescribe by general law within the limitations set forth in this section and Section 12 of this article.
Such political subdivisions shall have the power to incur indebtedness in the following categories and in no others:

(a) General obligation debt; and

(b) Indebtedness payable only from a revenue-producing project or from a special source as provided in subsection (10) of this section.

(3) "General obligation debt" shall mean any indebtedness of the political subdivision which shall be secured in whole or in part by a pledge of its full faith, credit and taxing power.

(4) General obligation debt may be incurred only for a purpose which is a public purpose and which is a corporate purpose of the applicable political subdivision. The power to incur general obligation debt shall include general obligation debt incurred by counties within the limitations prescribed by Section 12 of this article, and general obligation debt incurred by any political subdivision for purposes permitted by Section 13 of Article VIII of this Constitution. All general obligation debt shall mature within forty years from the time such indebtedness shall be incurred.

(5) No general obligation debt shall be incurred by any political subdivision unless prior to the delivery thereof a schedule showing the date and the principal and interest payments to become due thereon shall be filed in the office of the State Treasurer. If at any time any political subdivision shall fail to effect the punctual payment of the principal of or interest on its general obligation debt, then, in such instance, the State Treasurer shall withhold from such political subdivision sufficient moneys from any state appropriation to which such political subdivision may be entitled and apply so much as shall be necessary to the payment of the principal and interest on the indebtedness of the political subdivision then due. Any and all appropriations for political subdivisions of the State shall be subject to the provisions of this subsection.

(6) If general obligation debt be authorized by a majority vote of the qualified electors of the political subdivision voting in a referendum authorized by law, there shall be no conditions or restrictions limiting the incurring of such indebtedness except:

(a) those restrictions and limitations imposed in the authorization to incur such indebtedness;

(b) the provisions of subsection (4) hereof; and

(c) such general obligation debt shall be issued within five years of the date of such referendum.

(7) Subject to the provisions of subsection (4) of this section and on such terms and provisions as the General Assembly may, by general law, prescribe, general obligation debt may also be incurred by the governing body of each political subdivision:

(a) For any of its corporate purposes in an amount not exceeding eight percent of the assessed value of all taxable property of such political subdivision; or

(b) General obligation debt incurred pursuant to and within the limitations prescribed by Section 12 of this article.
In determining the debt limitations imposed by the provisions of subsection (7) of this section, bonded indebtedness incurred pursuant to the authorizations of subsection (6), bonded indebtedness existing on the date of this section becomes a part of the Constitution in 1977, and bonded indebtedness incurred pursuant to subsection (b) of this section, shall not be considered.

(8) General obligation debt may also be incurred in anticipation in the collection of ad valorem taxes or licenses (tax anticipation notes) under such terms and conditions as the General Assembly may prescribe by general law. Such tax anticipation notes shall be secured by a pledge of such taxes or license fees and a pledge of the full faith, credit and taxing power of the political subdivision. All tax anticipation notes shall be expressed to mature not later than ninety days from the date as of which such taxes or license fees may be paid without penalty.

(9) General obligation notes may also be issued in anticipation of the proceeds of general obligation bonds which may be lawfully issued (bond anticipation notes) under such terms and conditions that the General Assembly may prescribe by general law. Such bond anticipation notes shall be secured by a pledge of the proceeds of the bonds in anticipation of which such bond anticipation notes are issued and by a pledge of the full faith, credit and taxing power of the political subdivision.
Bond anticipation notes shall be expressed to mature not later than one year following the date of issuance, but if the General Assembly shall so authorize by law, bond anticipation notes may be refunded or renewed.

(10) Indebtedness payable solely from a revenue-producing project or from a special source, which source does not involve revenues from any tax or license, may be issued upon such terms and conditions as the General Assembly may prescribe by general law; provided, that the General Assembly may authorize by general law that indebtedness for the purpose of redevelopment within incorporated municipalities and counties may be incurred, and that the debt service of such indebtedness be provided from the added increments of tax revenues to result from any such project. Any and all indebtedness incurred pursuant to the provisions of this subsection shall contain a statement on the face thereof specifying the sources from which payment is to be made and shall state that the full faith, credit, and taxing powers are not pledged therefore.

Section 15. Bonded Indebtedness of School Districts

(1) The school districts of the State shall have the power to incur general obligation debt only in such manner and upon such terms and conditions as the General Assembly shall prescribe by law within the limitations set forth in this section.

(2) General obligation debt shall mean any indebtedness of the school district which shall be secured in whole or in part by a pledge of its full faith, credit and taxing power.

(3) General obligation debt may be incurred only for a purpose which is a public purpose and which is a corporate purpose of the applicable school district. The power to incur general obligation debt shall include general obligation debt incurred by any school districts for the purposes permitted by Section 13 of Article VIII of this Constitution. All general obligation debt shall mature within thirty years from the time such indebtedness shall be incurred.

(4) No general obligation debt shall be incurred by any school district unless prior to the delivery thereof a schedule showing the date and the principal and interest payments to become due thereon shall be filed in the office of the State Treasurer. If at any time any school district shall fail to effect the punctual payment of the principal and interest of its general obligation debt, the State Treasurer shall withhold from such school district sufficient moneys from any state appropriation to which such school district may be entitled and apply so much as shall be necessary to the payment of the principal and interest on the indebtedness of the school district then due. All appropriations for school districts of the State shall be subject to the provisions of this paragraph.

(5) If the general obligation debt be authorized by a majority vote of the qualified electors of the school district voting in a referendum authorized by law, there shall be no conditions or restrictions limiting the incurring of such indebtedness except:

(a) those restrictions and limitations imposed in the authorization to incur such indebtedness;

(b) such general obligation debt shall be issued within five years of the date of such referendum; and

(c) the provisions of subsection (3) hereof.

(6) In addition to the bonded indebtedness authorized by subsection (5), during the period beginning on the date of the ratification of this article in 1977 and ending on the fifth anniversary of that date, the governing body of any school district may incur bonded indebtedness to the limit authorized by Section 5, Article X of the Constitution as of January 1, 1976, and upon such terms and conditions as the General Assembly may have heretofore or may hereafter prescribe; provided, however, that in determining the limit authorized by Section 5, Article X of the Constitution, in the event the assessed value of all taxable property in any school district decreases in any year during the aforesaid five-year period to an amount less than the assessed value of all taxable property in any such school district as of December 31, 1975, the assessed value of all taxable property of any such school district as of December 31, 1975, shall be applied in determining any such school district's bonded indebtedness during the aforesaid five-year period. After the fifth anniversary of that date, the governing body of any school district may incur general obligation debt in an amount not exceeding eight percent of the assessed value of all taxable property of such school district subject to the provisions of subsection (3) of this section and upon such terms and conditions as the General Assembly may prescribe.
In computing the eight percent debt limitation imposed by the provisions of this subsection, bonded indebtedness existing on

the date of the fifth anniversary of the ratification of this article in 1977 and bonded indebtedness incurred under the provisions of subsection (5) of this section shall not be considered in the computation of the eight percent limitation.

(7) General obligation debt may also be incurred in anticipation of the collection of ad valorem taxes (tax anticipation notes) under such terms and conditions as the General Assembly may prescribe by law. Such tax anticipation notes shall be secured by a pledge of such taxes and a pledge of the full faith, credit and taxing power of the school district. All tax anticipation notes shall be expressed to mature not later than ninety days from the date as of which such taxes may be paid without penalty.

(8) General obligation notes may be issued in anticipation of the proceeds of general obligation bonds which may lawfully be issued (bond anticipation notes) under such terms and conditions that the General Assembly may prescribe by law. Such bond anticipation notes shall be secured by a pledge of the proceeds of the bonds in anticipation of which such bond anticipation notes are issued and by a pledge of the full faith, credit and taxing power of the school district.
Bond anticipation notes shall be expressed to mature not later than one year following the date of issuance, but if the General Assembly shall so authorize by law, bond anticipation notes may be refunded or renewed.

Section 16. Regulation of Benefits, Funding and Membership Contributions of State-Operated Retirement Systems; Investment of Funds

The governing body of any retirement or pension system in this State funded in whole or in part by public funds shall not pay any increased benefits to members or beneficiaries of such system above the benefit levels in effect on January 1, 1979, unless such governing body shall first determine that funding for such increase on a sound actuarial basis has been provided or is concurrently provided.

The General Assembly shall annually appropriate funds and prescribe member contributions for any state-operated retirement system which will insure the availability of funds to meet all normal and accrued liability of the system on a sound actuarial basis as determined by the governing body of the system.

Assets and funds established, created and accruing for the purpose of paying obligations to members of the several retirement systems of the State and political subdivisions shall not be diverted or used for any other purpose.

Notwithstanding the provisions of Section 11 of this article, the funds of the various state-operated retirement systems may be invested and reinvested in equity securities.

ARTICLE XI: PUBLIC EDUCATION

Section 1. State Board of Education

There shall be a State Board of Education composed of one member from each of the judicial circuits of the State. The members shall be elected by the legislative delegations of the several counties within each circuit for terms and with such powers and duties as may be provided by law and shall be rotated among the several counties. One additional member shall be appointed by the Governor. The members of the Board shall serve such terms and the Board shall have such powers and duties as the General Assembly shall specify by law.

Section 2. State Superintendent of Education

There shall be a State Superintendent of Education who shall be the chief administrative officer of the public education system of the State and shall have such qualifications as may be prescribed by law.

Section 3. System of Free Public Schools and Other Public Institutions of Learning

The General Assembly shall provide for the maintenance and support of a system of free public schools open to all children in the State and shall establish, organize and support such other public institutions of learning, as may be desirable.

Section 4. Direct Aid to Religious or Other Private Educational Institutions Prohibited

No money shall be paid from public funds nor shall the credit of the State or any of its political subdivisions be used for the direct benefit of any religious or other private educational institution.

ARTICLE XII: FUNCTIONS OF GOVERNMENT

Section 1. Matters of Public Concern; General Assembly to Provide Appropriate Agencies

The health, welfare, and safety of the lives and property of the people of this State and the conservation of its natural resources are matters of public concern. The General Assembly shall provide appropriate agencies to function in these areas of public concern and determine the activities, powers, and duties of such agencies.

Section 2. Institutions for Confinement of Persons Convicted of Crimes

The General Assembly shall establish institutions for the confinement of all persons convicted of such crimes as may be designated by law, and shall provide for the custody, maintenance, health, welfare, education, and rehabilitation of the inmates.

Section 3. Separate Confinement of Juvenile Offenders

The General Assembly shall provide for the separate confinement of juvenile offenders under the age of seventeen from older confined persons.

Section 4. Reserved

Section 5. Reserved

Section 6. Reserved

Section 7. Reserved

Section 8. Reserved

Section 9. Control of Convicts

The Penitentiary and the convicts thereto sentenced shall forever be under the supervision and control of officers employed by the State; and in case any convicts are hired or farmed out, as may be provided by law, their maintenance, support, medical attendance and discipline shall be under the direction of officers detailed for those duties by the authorities of the Penitentiary. Provided, however, that the General Assembly may authorize the Department of Corrections to transfer inmates to correctional institutions of other states or the federal government for confinement, treatment or rehabilitation when such transfers are deemed to be in the best interest of the inmate concerned.

ARTICLE XIII: MILITIA

Section 1. Militia

The militia of this State shall consist of all able-bodied male citizens of the State between the ages of eighteen and forty-five years, except such persons as are now or may be exempted by the laws of the United States or this State, or who from religious scruples may be adverse to bearing arms, and shall be organized, officered, armed, equipped and disciplined as the General Assembly may by law direct.

Section 2. When Exempt from Arrest

The volunteer and militia forces shall (except for treason, felony and breach of the peace) be exempt from arrest by warrant or other process while in active service or attending muster or the election of officers, or while going to or returning from either of the same.

Section 3. Governor May Call Out

The Governor shall have the power to call out the volunteer and militia forces, either or both, to execute the laws, repel invasions, suppress insurrections and preserve the public peace.

Section 4. Adjutant and Inspector General; Staff Officers

There must be an Adjutant General. The position of Adjutant General is recognized as holding the rank of Major General, and the Adjutant General's duties and compensation must be prescribed by law. The Governor, by and with the advice and consent of the Senate, shall appoint staff officers as the General Assembly may direct.

Beginning upon the expiration of the term of the Adjutant General serving in office on the date of the ratification of the provisions of this paragraph, the Adjutant General must be appointed by the Governor, with the advice and consent of the Senate, in the manner provided in Section 7, Article VI.

Section 5. Confederate Pensions

The General Assembly is hereby empowered and required, at its first session after the adoption of this Constitution, to provide such proper and liberal legislation as will guarantee and secure an annual pension to every indigent or disabled Confederate soldier and sailor of this State and of the late Confederate States who are citizens of this State, and also to the indigent widows of Confederate soldiers and sailors.

ARTICLE XIV: EMINENT DOMAIN

Section 1. Boundary Rivers

The State shall have concurrent jurisdiction on all rivers bordering on this State, so far as such rivers shall form a common boundary to this and any other State bounded by the same; and they, together with all navigable waters within the limits of the State, shall be common highways and forever free, as well to the inhabitants of this State as to the citizens of the United States, without any tax or impost therefore, unless the same be expressly provided for by the General Assembly.

Section 2. Title to Certain Lands

The title to all lands and other property which have heretofore accrued to this State by grant, gift, purchase, forfeiture, escheats or otherwise shall vest in the State of South Carolina, the same as though no change had taken place.

Section 3. Ultimate Property in Lands

The people of the State are declared to possess the ultimate property in and to all lands within the jurisdiction of the State; and all lands the title to which shall fail from defect of heirs shall revert or escheat to the people.

Section 4. Navigable Waters Free; Tax for Use of Wharf

All navigable waters shall forever remain public highways free to the citizens of the State and the United States without tax, impost or toll imposed; and no tax, toll, impost or wharfage shall be imposed, demanded or received from the owners of any merchandise or commodity for the use of the shores or any wharf erected on the shores or in or over the waters of any navigable stream unless the same be authorized by the General Assembly.

Section 5. Reserved

ARTICLE XV: IMPEACHMENT

Section 1. Power of Impeachment; Vote Required; Suspension of Officer Impeached

The House of Representatives alone shall have the power of impeachment in cases of serious crimes or serious misconduct in office by officials elected on a statewide basis, state judges, and such other state officers as may be designated by law. The affirmative vote of two-thirds of all members elected shall be required for an impeachment. Any officer impeached shall thereby be suspended from office until judgment in the case shall have been pronounced, and the office shall be filled during the trial in such manner as may be provided by law.

Section 2. Trial of Impeachments; Judgment; Proceedings No Bar to Criminal Prosecution; Impeachment of Governor

All impeachments shall be tried by the Senate, and when sitting for that purpose Senators shall be under oath or affirmation. No person shall be convicted except by a vote of two-thirds of all members elected. Judgment in such case shall be limited to removal from office. Impeachment proceedings, whether or not resulting in conviction, shall not be a bar to criminal prosecution and punishment according to law.

When the Governor is impeached, the Chief Justice of the Supreme Court, or, if he be disqualified, the Senior Justice, shall preside, with a casting vote in all preliminary questions.

Section 3. Removal of Officers by Governor on Address of General Assembly

For any willful neglect of duty, or other reasonable cause, which shall not be sufficient ground of impeachment, the Governor shall remove any executive or judicial officer on the address of two thirds of each house of the General Assembly: Provided, that the cause or causes for which said removal may be required shall be stated at length in such address, and entered on the Journals of each house: And, provided, further, that the officer intended to be removed shall be notified of such cause or causes, and shall be admitted to a hearing in his own defense, or by his counsel, or by both, before any vote for such address; and in all cases the vote shall be taken by yeas and nays, and be entered on the Journal of each house respectively.

ARTICLE XVI: AMENDMENT AND
REVISION OF THE CONSTITUTION

Section 1. Amendments

Any amendment or amendments to this Constitution may be proposed in the Senate or House of Representatives. However, for the general election in 1990, revision of an entire article or the addition of a new article may be proposed as a single amendment with only one question being required to be submitted to the electors. The amendment may delete, revise, and transpose provisions from other articles of the Constitution provided the provisions are germane to the subject matter of the article being revised or being proposed. If it is agreed to by two-thirds of the members elected to each House, the amendment or amendments must be entered on the Journals respectively, with the yeas and nays taken on it and must be submitted to the qualified electors of the State at the next general election for Representatives. If a majority of the electors qualified to vote for members of the General Assembly voting on the question vote in favor of the amendment or amendments and a majority of each branch of the next General Assembly, after the election and before another, ratify the amendment or amendments, by yeas and nays, they become part of the Constitution. The amendment or amendments must be read three times, on three several days, in each House.

Section 2. Two or More Amendments

If two or more amendments shall be submitted at the same time, they shall be submitted in such manner that the electors shall vote for or against each of such amendments separately.

Section 3. Constitutional Convention

Whenever two-thirds of the members elected to each branch of the General Assembly shall think it necessary to call a Convention to revise, amend or change this Constitution, they shall recommend to the electors to vote for or against a Convention at the next election for Representatives; and if a majority of all the electors voting at said election shall have voted for a Convention, the General Assembly shall, at its next session, provide by law for calling the same; and such Convention shall consist of a number of members equal to that of the most numerous branch of the General Assembly.

ARTICLE XVII: MISCELLANEOUS MATTERS

Section 1. Qualifications of Officers

No person shall be elected or appointed to any office in this State unless he possess the qualifications of an elector: Provided, The provisions of this Section shall not apply to the offices of State Librarian and Departmental Clerks, to either of which offices any woman, a resident of the State two years, who has attained the age of twenty-one years, shall be eligible.

Section 1A. Qualification for Office; Dual Office Holding

Every qualified elector is eligible to any office to be voted for, unless disqualified by age, as prescribed in this Constitution. No person may hold two offices of honor or profit at the same time, but any person holding another office may at the same time be an officer in the militia, member of a lawfully and regularly organized fire department, constable, or a notary public. The limitation above set forth "No person may hold two offices of honor or profit at the same time," does not apply to the circuit judges of the State under the circumstances stated in this section, but whenever it appears that any or all of the Justices of the Supreme Court are disqualified or otherwise prevented from presiding in any cause for the reasons set forth in Section 6 of Article V of the Constitution, the Chief Justice or in his stead the Senior Associate Justice when available shall designate the requisite number of circuit judges for the hearing and determination of the hearing. The limitation above set forth does not prohibit any officeholder from being a delegate to a constitutional convention.

Section 1B. Property Qualifications; Term of Office; Dueling

No property qualification, unless prescribed in this Constitution, shall be necessary for an election to or the holding of any office. No person shall be elected or appointed to office in this State for life or during good behavior, but the terms of all officers shall be for some specified period, except Notaries Public and officers in the Militia. After the adoption of this Constitution any person who shall fight a duel or send or accept a challenge for that purpose, or be an aider or abettor in fighting a duel, shall be deprived of holding any office of honor or trust in this State, and shall be otherwise punished as the law shall prescribe.

Section 2. Claims Against State

The General Assembly may direct, by law, in what manner claims against the State may be established and adjusted.

Section 3. Divorces

Divorces from the bonds of matrimony shall be allowed on the grounds of adultery, desertion, physical cruelty, continuous separation for a period of at least one year or habitual drunkenness.

Section 4. Supreme Being

No person who denies the existence of a Supreme Being shall hold any office under this Constitution.

Section 5. Public Printing

The printing of the laws, journals, bills, legislative documents and papers for each branch of the General Assembly, with the printing required for the Executive and other departments of the State, shall be done as provided by law.

Section 6. Removal of Causes

The General Assembly shall provide for the removal of all causes which may be pending when this Constitution goes into effect to Courts created by the same.

Section 7. Lotteries

Only the State may conduct lotteries, and these lotteries must be conducted in the manner that the General Assembly provides by law. The revenue derived from the lotteries must first be used to pay all operating expenses and prizes for the lotteries. The remaining lottery revenues must be credited to a separate fund in the state treasury styled the 'Education Lottery Account', and the earnings on this account must be credited to it. Education Lottery Account proceeds may be used only for education purposes as the General Assembly provides by law.

The game of bingo, when conducted by charitable, religious, or fraternal organizations exempt from federal income taxation or when conducted at recognized annual state and county fairs, is not considered a lottery prohibited by this section.

A raffle, if provided for by general law and conducted by a nonprofit organization for charitable, religious, fraternal, educational, or other eleemosynary purposes is not a lottery prohibited by this section. The general law must define the type of nonprofit organization authorized to operate and conduct a raffle, provide standards for the operation and conduct of raffles, provide for the use of proceeds for religious, charitable, fraternal, educational, or other eleemosynary purposes, provide penalties for violations, and provide for other laws necessary to ensure the proper functioning, honesty, and integrity of the raffles. If no general law on the conduct and operation of a nonprofit raffle for charitable purposes, including the type of organization allowed to conduct raffles, is enacted, then the raffle is a lottery prohibited by this section.

Section 7B. Special Election for Bonding Municipality

In authorizing a special election in any incorporated city or town in this State for the purpose of bonding the same, the General Assembly shall prescribe as a condition precedent to the holding of said election a petition from a majority of the freeholders of said city or town as shown by its tax books, and at such elections all electors of such city or town who are duly qualified for voting under Section 12 of this Article, and who have paid all taxes, State, County and municipal, for the previous year, shall be allowed to vote; and the vote of a majority of those voting in said election shall be necessary to authorize the issue of said bonds.

Provided, That the General Assembly need not prescribe any such petition as a condition precedent to the holding of any such election in the City of Columbia, where the proceeds of the bonds are authorized to be used solely for the purpose of enlarging, extending and repairing a sewerage system and plant or a waterworks system and plant, or for the purchase, building and maintenance of fire stations, fire alarm systems and fire equipment, or for any one or more of said purposes.

Provided, further, That the limitations imposed by this Section and by Section 5 of Article X of the Constitution shall not apply to any bonded indebtedness incurred by the City of Columbia, where the bonded indebtedness is authorized to be incurred for the purpose of enlarging and maintaining its fire department or for purchase, building and maintenance of fire stations, fire alarm systems or fire equipment, or for any one or more of said purposes and when the question of incurring such bonded indebtedness is submitted to the qualified electors of said City at an election or elections to be called by the City Council of said City, and a majority of those voting thereon shall vote in favor thereof; and the General Assembly need not prescribe as a condition precedent to the holding of any such election a petition from the freeholders as provided in Section 13 of Article II of the Constitution.

Provided, That the General Assembly need not prescribe any such petition as a condition precedent to the holding of any such election in the City of Myrtle Beach where the proceeds of the bonds are authorized to be used solely for the purpose of enlarging, extending and improving the waterworks system or the sewage disposal system.

Provided, that the General Assembly need not prescribe any such petition of freeholders as a condition precedent to the holding of any such election in the City of Columbia where the proceeds of the bonds to be authorized are used for any corporate purpose of the City of Columbia. It is intended that the term "City of Columbia" as used in this amendment shall mean the City of Columbia with corporate limits as now constituted or as hereafter altered following merger, annexation, or modification of corporate limits.

Provided, that the General Assembly need not prescribe any such petition of freeholders as a condition precedent to the holding of any such election in the City of Charleston where the proceeds of the bonds to be authorized are used for any corporate purpose of the City of Charleston. It is intended that the term "City of Charleston" as used in this amendment shall mean the City of Charleston with corporate limits as now constituted or as hereafter altered following merger, annexation, or modification of corporate limits.

Provided, that the General Assembly need not prescribe any such petition of freeholders as a condition precedent to the holding of any such election in the City of Greenville where the proceeds of the bonds to be authorized are used for any corporate purpose of the City of Greenville. It is intended that the term "City of Greenville" as used in this amendment shall mean the City of Greenville with corporate limits as now constituted or as hereafter altered following merger, annexation, or modification of corporate limits.

Provided, that provisions of this section prescribing the petition of freeholders as a condition precedent to the holding of any such election shall not apply to the City of Spartanburg where the proceeds of the bonds to be authorized are used for any corporate purpose of the City of Spartanburg. It is intended that the term "City of Spartanburg" as used in this amendment shall mean the City of Spartanburg with corporate limits as now constituted or as hereafter altered following merger, annexation, or modification of corporate limits.

Provided, that the provisions of this section requiring a petition of the freeholders and the holding of an election shall not apply to any obligation incurred by the City of Florence to Florence County or to any agency of Florence County resulting from a long-term lease of a portion of a multistoried office building to be erected by Florence County for the purpose of providing courthouse, jail, city hall, office and related facilities for Florence County and for the City of Florence and for other governmental agencies, pursuant to which the full faith and credit of the City of Florence is pledged to the payment of rent and other obligations under such lease.

Provided, that the General Assembly need not prescribe any such petition of freeholders as a condition precedent to the holding of any such election in the City of Greer where the proceeds of the bonds to be authorized are used for any corporate purpose of the City of Greer. It is intended that the term "City of Greer" as used in this amendment shall mean the City of Greer with corporate limits as now constituted or as hereafter altered following merger, annexation, or modification of corporate limits.

Provided, that provisions of this section prescribing the petition of freeholders as a condition precedent to the holding of any such election shall not apply to any incorporated municipality located in York County where the proceeds of the bonds to be authorized are used for any corporate purpose of such municipality. It is intended that the term "Incorporated municipality in York County" as used in this amendment shall mean all incorporated municipalities now existing or hereafter created, and as originally constituted or as afterwards altered following merger, annexation, or modification of corporate limits.

Section 8. Officers Gambling and Betting

It shall be unlawful for any person holding an office of honor, trust or profit to engage in gambling or betting on games of chance; and any such officer, upon conviction thereof, shall become thereby disqualified from the further exercise of the functions of his office, and the office of said person shall become vacant, as in the case of resignation or death.

Section 9. Property of Married Women

The real and personal property of a woman held at the time of her marriage, or that which she may thereafter acquire, either by gift, grant, inheritance, devise or otherwise, shall be her separate property, and she shall have all the rights incident to the same to which an unmarried woman or a man is entitled. She shall have the power to contract and be contracted with in the same manner as if she were unmarried.

Section 10. Laws Now in Force

All laws now in force in this State and not repugnant to this Constitution shall remain and be enforced until altered or repealed by the General Assembly, or shall expire by their own limitations.

Section 11. Schedule

That no inconvenience may arise from the change in the Constitution of this State, and in order to carry this Constitution into complete operation, it is hereby declared:

First. Laws Now of Force; Ordinances

That all laws in force in this State, at the time of the adoption of this Constitution, not inconsistent therewith, and constitutional when enacted shall remain in full force until altered or repealed by the General Assembly or expire by their own limitation. All ordinances passed and ratified at this Convention shall have the same force and effect as if included in and constituting a part of this Constitution.

Second. Writs, Actions, etc

All writs, actions, causes of action, proceedings, prosecutions and rights of individuals, of bodies corporate and of the State, when not inconsistent with this Constitution, shall continue as valid.

Third. Laws Inconsistent with Constitution

The provisions of all laws which are inconsistent with this Constitution shall cease upon its adoption, except that all laws which are inconsistent with such provisions of this Constitution as require legislation to enforce them shall remain in force until such legislation is had.

Fourth. Fines, etc., Accruing

All fines, penalties, forfeitures and escheats accruing to the State of South Carolina under the Constitution and laws heretofore in force shall accrue to the use of the State of South Carolina under this Constitution, except as herein otherwise provided.

Fifth. Recognizances, etc.; Indictments

All recognizances, obligations and all other instruments entered into or executed before the adoption of this Constitution to the State, or to any County, township, city or town therein, and all fines, taxes, penalties and forfeitures due or owing to this State, or to any County, township, city or town therein, and all writs, prosecutions, actions and proceedings, except as herein otherwise provided, shall continue and remain unaffected by the adoption of this Constitution. All indictments which shall have been found, or may hereafter be found, for any crime or offence committed before the adoption of this Constitution may be prosecuted as if no change had been made, except as otherwise provided herein.

Sixth. All Officers Hold Over; Compensation

All officers, State, executive, legislative, judicial, circuit, district, County, township and municipal, who may be in office at the adoption of this Constitution, or who may be elected before the election of their successors as herein provided, shall hold their respective offices until their terms have expired and until their successors are elected or appointed and qualified as provided in this Constitution, unless sooner removed as may be provided by law; and shall receive the compensation now fixed by the Statute Laws in force at the adoption of this Constitution.

Seventh. Elections

At all elections held for members of the General Assembly in case of a vacancy, or for any other office, State, County or municipal, the qualifications of electors shall remain as they were under the Constitution of Eighteen hundred and Sixty-eight until the first day of November, in the year Eighteen hundred and Ninety-six.

Eighth. Takes Effect

This Constitution, adopted by the people of South Carolina in Convention assembled, shall be in force and effect from and after the Thirty-first day of December, in the year Eighteen hundred and Ninety-five.

Ninth. Constitution of 1868 Repealed

The provisions of the Constitution of Eighteen hundred and Sixty-eight and amendments thereto are repealed by this Constitution, except when re-ordained and declared herein.

Section 12. Continuity of Governmental Operation During Enemy Attack

The General Assembly, in order to insure continuity of state and local governmental operations in periods of emergency resulting from disasters caused by enemy attack, shall have the power and the immediate duty:

(1) to provide for prompt and temporary succession to the powers and duties of public offices, of whatever nature and whether filled by election or appointment, the incumbents of which may become unavailable for carrying on the powers and duties of such offices, and

(2) to adopt such other measures as may be necessary and proper for insuring the continuity of governmental operations. In the exercise of the powers hereby conferred, the General Assembly shall in all respects conform to the requirements of this Constitution, except to the extent that in the judgment of the General Assembly so to do would be impracticable or would admit of undue delay.

Section 13. Use of Funds Realized by Greenwood County from Sale of Electric Properties and System

Funds realized by Greenwood County from the sale of its electric properties and system shall be held intact as an investment fund. Only investments in securities permitted by law may be made and then only by the governing body of the county. No portion of the principal amount of the fund shall be used for any other purpose.

Section 14. Citizens Deemed Sui Juris; Restrictions as to Sale of Alcoholic Beverages

Every citizen who is eighteen years of age or older, not laboring under disabilities prescribed in this Constitution or otherwise established by law, shall be deemed sui juris and endowed with full legal rights and responsibilities, provided, that the General Assembly may restrict the sale of alcoholic beverages to persons until age twenty-one.

Section 15. Lawful Domestic Unions Recognizable in State; Domestic Unions Created in Another Jurisdiction

A marriage between one man and one woman is the only lawful domestic union that shall be valid or recognized in this State. This State and its political subdivisions shall not create a legal status, right, or claim respecting any other domestic union, however denominated. This State and its political subdivisions shall not recognize or give effect to a legal status, right, or claim created by another jurisdiction respecting any other domestic union, however denominated. Nothing in this section shall impair any right or benefit extended by the State or its political subdivisions other than a right or benefit arising from a domestic union that is not valid or recognized in this State. This section shall not prohibit or limit parties, other than the State or its political subdivisions, from entering into contracts or other legal instruments.